MONTEVERDI IN OLD AGE
From the title-page of Marinoni's 'Fiori Poetici'

MONTEVERDI

by

DENIS ARNOLD

*With eight pages of plates
and music examples in the text*

LONDON
J. M. DENT AND SONS LTD

FARRAR, STRAUS AND CUDAHY INC.
NEW YORK

© Text, J. M. Dent & Sons Ltd, 1963

All rights reserved
Made in Great Britain
at the
Aldine Press · Letchworth · Herts
for
J. M. DENT & SONS LTD
Aldine House · Bedford Street · London
First published 1963

PREFACE

Two STUDIES of Monteverdi's life and works, both based on recent research, are available in English. The preface for a third one must necessarily be an explanation for writing yet another. The main reason is simply that a series such as the Master Musicians can no longer neglect Monteverdi, whose greatness is now generally acknowledged; and the need for a book designed specifically for the English general reader is increased because the existing books were both intended for a somewhat different audience. Professor Schrade's *Monteverdi: the Creator of Modern Music*, with its detailed analyses, is best read with the complete edition to hand; Professor Redlich's *Claudio Monteverdi: Life and Works* was written originally for the German reader with a knowledge of Heinrich Schütz and Samuel Scheidt rather than for the Englishman who knows Byrd and Wilbye.

I have therefore tried to write a study which will introduce Monteverdi and his background to readers with a limited knowledge of Italian music of the time. In the musical examples the filling in of the *continuo* part has been made as simple as possible, both to save space and to facilitate performance. It in no way represents my views on the method to be used in the performance of Monteverdi's work. The time-values of certain examples have been reduced to conform with modern notation. The bibliography is also a guide for the general reader rather than for the scholar.

Bearing this in mind, I have deliberately avoided marshalling all the arguments about such matters as the authenticity of *Il ritorno d'Ulisse* and the meaning of *canto alla francese*. But in one matter I have ventured to state my views at some length. Previous writers have all stressed the revolutionary nature of Monteverdi's music. After a fairly

Preface

close examination of music by certain of his contemporaries, it seemed to me to be more accurate to consider him as a moderate and progressive rather than an experimental composer. Since the music of these other composers is not widely known, I have tried to give sufficient background material to justify this new approach, though not, I hope, at such great length that it distorts the broader picture which the general reader requires.

Extracts from Einstein, *Essays on Music*, and Strunk, *Source Readings in Music History*, are by kind permission of Faber & Faber Ltd (London) and W. W. Norton & Co. Inc. (New York).

Two engravings of Venetian scenes are reproduced by permission of the Trustees of the Victoria and Albert Museum. I have to thank my colleagues Professor Philip Cranmer, Mr Raymond Warren and Mr R. H. Semple for reading either the whole or part of this book in manuscript and making some most helpful suggestions; Dr G. B. Gaidoni for checking the translations from Italian; Mr Gordon Wheeler for reading the proofs with a splendidly keen eye and compiling the index; and my wife, who not only typed the book from an illegible manuscript, but encouraged me to finish it.

D. A.

Belfast,
September 1962.

CONTENTS

ILLUSTRATIONS

CHAPTER I

CREMONA

'IT IS a beautiful and large town, whose precincts are at least 5,000 steps, surrounded by fine walls and defended by a castle which is very strong. . . . The houses of Cremona are beautiful, large and well constructed, so that one could say that all of them are palaces. There are several public squares, all very beautiful. The streets are wide and straight, and there are several beautiful public gardens in the town.'[1] In this way an eighteenth-century French writer describes Cremona, where Monteverdi was born. The town lies on the banks of the river Po, about fifty miles from Milan, in the heart of the great plain of northern Italy. It is a place comparatively unvisited today, except by tourists who wish to look at the cathedral and the splendidly tall clock tower. Indeed it seems an almost isolated town, distant from all the major cities of Italy with the exception of Milan, not even on a main road to the east or south.

Yet in the sixteenth century it was a good place for the musician or artist to be born in. If in itself Cremona was too small and too provincial to be very important, it was near several centres of Renaissance society. Milan, dominated by the Spaniard, was the least interesting of these. Parma, whose ruling family, the Farnese, was linked strongly with the Netherlands, was more important and provided a fitting setting for several great composers, including Cipriano de Rore and Merulo. Mantua, to the east, was ruled by the Gonzagas, rich, prosperous and cultured, for they too liked good music and painting. A little farther away were Ferrara, the most progressive court, musically speaking, in Europe; Venice, more conservative, but the heart of music publishing and full of fine composers, players and painters;

[1] *Les Délices de l'Italie*, Tome iv (Paris, 1707).

1

Florence; and the Transalpine courts of Bavaria, Innsbruck and Graz. This region in northern Italy, its ground fertile to the point of luxury, was the heart of artistic Europe, the equivalent of eighteenth-century Vienna or nineteenth-century Paris.

We are not sure of the exact day when Monteverdi was born. The first record to be found is of his baptism, which took place on 15th May 1567. He was the eldest child of Baldasar Monteverdi, a doctor, whose wife Maddalena gave birth to four more children, two of them girls. We know nothing of his earliest years. All that we can say is that his family must have been musical, since of the boys, both Claudio and his brother Giulio Cesare became professional musicians. It is usually assumed that Claudio became a choirboy in Cremona Cathedral, and this seems likely enough if we consider the musical institutions in a small town of the period.

Lacking the natural focusing point of patronage which a prince and his retinue provided for larger cities, the most important centre of music-making was undoubtedly the principal church of the town, usually the cathedral. This would normally have a small choir of about ten men and up to fifteen boys. Some of the men may also have played instruments, but the only professional player would be the organist. At the head of these was a director of music, or *maestro di cappella*. The cathedral chapter tried to find a composer for this post, since he was expected to provide music for the more important festivals. He was also expected to conduct the choir, and to instruct both priests and boys in the art of music. The priests for the most part only learned to sing plainsong. The boys, on the other hand, received a complete education in music, as well as being given the elements of a literary education by a teacher called the *maestro de grammatica*.

Compared with court musicians, the servants of the church were not very well paid, but they were comfortably enough off and a modest social status was accorded to them. Further down the social ladder were the town musicians, or *piffari*. These were wind-players, and were employed by the municipality for various purposes. They entertained the populace in the town square, as Montaigne found at Piacenza (in the Duchy of Parma, not far from Cremona) and wrote in his journal:

CREMONA CATHEDRAL
From Antonio Campo's 'Historia di Cremona'

'Morning and night they play for one hour on those instruments we call oboes, but which they call *piffari*!' At other times they accompanied the mayor and town dignitaries in processions to church. In some towns they had to teach anyone who wanted to learn an instrument. For such duties they were paid very badly, though in the end they probably made enough money from casual engagements—playing at weddings and banquets, or in church when hired by the *maestro di cappella* for a festival. Socially they were usually considered a cut below the more dignified musicians of church and court, but they were men of considerable skill. Some of them could play virtually any wind instrument and sing as well. Entry into their ranks was usually by apprenticeship, and in the manner of the guilds they were strict in the upkeep of their standards.

Finally, the musician could sometimes gain an education and a livelihood from the academies which were so important in the sixteenth century. These were not teaching institutions. They were associations of upper-class gentlemen who wished to discuss literary topics, learn a little music or otherwise follow the curriculum laid down by the courtesy books such as Castiglione's *The Courtier*. Some of these academies paid musicians quite well to instruct and entertain their members. Others employed them more casually. But whether employed full-time or not, these musicians were generally more intelligent and better educated than those of church or town. Their patrons often discussed the basic philosophy of music with them, and at least in some of them there was a very close relationship between musician and gentry.

Monteverdi must have learned his music from the church and its seminary. A boy from a doctor's family would never have been apprenticed to a town musician. And although we know that there was an academy in Cremona, Monteverdi was too accomplished a musician at a very early age to have picked up his knowledge amongst amateurs, for at the age of fifteen he was ready to publish a book of motets with the distinguished Venetian publishing firm of Gardano. The title-page tells us that they are sacred songs for three voices and that the composer is a pupil of Marc' Antonio Ingegneri. Ingegneri, whose pupil Monteverdi was proud to acknowledge himself, was *maestro di cappella* at Cremona Cathedral. He was exactly the kind of man we should expect to find there. Educated (perhaps also born) in Verona, he started as a singer at Cremona before being promoted to be director of music. He had published some madrigals and church music by the time Monteverdi produced the *Sacrae cantiunculae*, and these reveal him as a sound rather than brilliant composer, inclining to the older methods of contrapuntal music which we associate with the Netherlands composers. Nevertheless he was not completely old-fashioned. He knew something of the newer style of Cipriano de Rore, and he must have been a good teacher, for Monteverdi's pieces show every sign of proficiency.

It is not surprising that a choirboy should set Latin words rather than attempt the madrigal style straight away; nor that this book was for three voices, which are easier to manipulate than the five or six voices usual for motets at this time. What is a little surprising, perhaps, is that the book appeared under the imprint of the most famous Venetian publisher, especially since the dedication is to a priest and not to a member of the nobility who might have provided a subsidy. The reason for Gardano's acceptance may well have been the easiness of the music for the performer, and the fact that it was suitable for domestic devotional singing as well as for churches with very small choirs. In any case we find Monteverdi continuing in this vein, for in the next year he produced a set of *madrigali spirituali* for four voices— again no mean achievement for a boy not yet sixteen. This time he had to rest content with a less distinguished publisher in Brescia, and since the dedication is to a Cremonese nobleman, this book almost certainly was subsidized. Continuing his career as a prodigy, Monteverdi in his eighteenth year saw yet another book in print. This time it was a book which broke away from the ecclesiastical traditions—a book of canzonets for three voices. This was a popular *genre* at the time, and the book was likely to sell. Monteverdi tried yet another publisher in Venice, the house of Vincenti and Amadino, which accepted the work. Whether they made any money out of it we shall never know, but Amadino's shrewdness was continually to profit him, for he published most of Monteverdi's later music, including the very popular books of madrigals which went through many editions.

Then comes a gap of three years in our knowledge of Monteverdi's life and works. Some writers have surmised that he attended the University of Cremona, but there is no evidence for this—rather the reverse, in fact, for later in life he was to say that he never understood the antique signs and notations of the Greeks, something about which he would surely have been less modest if he had had a normal education in classical thought. Certainly there is little evidence that he was widely read, or that his knowledge of the classical philosophers was any more than he might have obtained in discussions with members of an academy. It is more probable that he continued his studies to be a professional musician; on the title-page of his next book, his first book of madrigals, he still proclaims himself a pupil of Ingegneri. The dedication is again to a member of Cremona's nobility, Count Marco Verita, and so experienced does Monteverdi seem by this time that we are a little surprised to find in it a modest declaration: 'I must not expect for compositions so much the product of youth, such as are these of mine, other praise than that which can be given to the flowers of spring in comparison with those awarded to the fruits of summer and autumn.' Monteverdi was nineteen and had published four books in a little over four years. He was evidently an ambitious young man; we may note that in the secure surroundings of his later life he never published his work so eagerly.

His ambitions were certainly not to be fulfilled in his home town, and like other composers from Cremona he began to think of leaving it. Benedetto Pallavicino was now at the Mantuan court; so was Gastoldi, who had left nearby Caravaggio. Costanzo Porta had gone away to Padua, Massaino to Prague and Salzburg. All had improved their position by leaving Cremona; and the style of Monteverdi's madrigal book shows that now he could learn little more from Ingegneri. His first attempt at finding a post away from home apparently was directed towards Milan. His father had had dealings with the Milanese health authorities as the representative of the Cremona Doctors' Association and no doubt had friends there. Claudio

Monteverdi went up to the city in 1589 and tried to obtain the influence of Giacomo Riccardi, then President of His Catholic Majesty's most excellent Senate and Council in Milan. He was unsuccessful—luckily, since Milan, under the influence of the foreigner, was a backwater at this time and remained so during the seventeenth century. He seems to have made some friends who were to help him in his Mantuan years, but for the time being he had to return to Cremona.

Back there, he put his energies into the preparation of a second book of madrigals, which came out in the following year. This was dedicated to Riccardi, perhaps in the hope that something might still turn up in Milan. This madrigal book still acknowledges the teaching of Ingegneri on the title-page: its contents do not. On the contrary, the mature style of these madrigals reveals more clearly that Monteverdi was looking far beyond the confines of Cremona, and was studying the works of more famous and more modern masters than his old teacher.

The exact date, and even the year itself, when Monteverdi left Cremona are unknown to us. In one of his letters written in 1608 he writes of his nineteen years' service in Mantua, which, if true, means that he must have started his life there as early as 1589. Another of his letters, written in 1615, speaks of his 'twenty-one years of service in Mantua', and since he was deprived of his post there in 1612, this suggests that he went to his new post in 1591. Against this must be placed the fact that a list of musicians compiled by the treasurer at the Mantuan court in this later year [1] does not contain the name of Monteverdi. Perhaps the most reasonable explanation is that he went to Mantua in the two or three earlier years to take occasional and part-time engagements, of which there were plenty to be had, and then was given a permanent place in the latter part of 1591. Of one thing we can be certain. By the time he was ready to publish yet another madrigal book in 1592 he was *suonatore di vivuola* to Vincenzo I, Duke of Mantua, and in his first permanent post.

[1] Arch. Gonzaga *Busta* 395.

CHAPTER II

THE visitor to Mantua may find it hard to believe how great was Monteverdi's success. The town today seems rather forlorn, its huge palace a museum, its present *raison d'être* a market for the rich country-side by which it is surrounded. In the later years of the sixteenth century it was very different. Although never destined to be one of the greatest cities of Europe, Mantua was no mere provincial centre. The house of Gonzaga had brought the city to a fine prosperity, and encouraged by a succession of dukes who loved all the outward signs of richness, artists and musicians, actors and poets were glad to accept the bountiful patronage they were offered. Rubens, Tasso and Guarini are only three among many famous names in letters and painting that we find associated with the Mantuan court; and to these can be added a group of musicians just as distinguished.

By a singular act of good fortune, the prosperity of Mantua was assured by the sagacity of a duke who was both cultured and thoroughly educated. Duke Guglielmo, who came into power in 1550, had a flair for organization and was progressive in his methods of government. Tasso could write of him that he was 'a prince of high talent and culture and most just and liberal'. Under him Mantua achieved a rare stability, and music was perhaps his greatest love. Not content with being a patron of musicians, he was a composer himself and sent his compositions to Palestrina for comment and correction. It was not his fault that Mantua's music was not directed by Palestrina or Marenzio; both were too comfortable elsewhere. As it was, Giaches de Wert was Guglielmo's *maestro di cappella*, and he built up a group of musicians among the most famous of the age. Alessandro Striggio, Gastoldi, Pallavicino and Soriano were all well-known composers;

Gastoldi and Wert indeed were world famous. Rome or Venice apart, Mantua's musicians could not be surpassed.

If Guglielmo was something near to the ideal of a Renaissance monarch, his son, who became Duke Vincenzo I in 1587, was nearer the normal. Fond of women and gambling, he was in his youth at best an inconsiderate and inconsistent ruler, at the worst a brute and a murderer. He had no compunction about divorcing his first wife, accusing her publicly of physical deformity; and when the counter charge of his impotence was made by her family, proposed a trial of his virility on a virgin girl in Venice. Yet he could be genuinely repentant, giving vast sums to churches and monasteries, or planning a pilgrimage to the holy places in Palestine (although this was prevented by his death). He also supported artists of all kinds. The ducal palace was further embellished in his lifetime. Music was encouraged, and drama was almost a passion with him. Was it a production of *Il pastor fido* by Guarini in 1591 which provided Monteverdi with one of his first engagements in Mantua? The music for this play was composed by Giaches de Wert, and the production was planned on a most sumptuous scale, to be given in the courtyard of the Palazzo del Tè. The customary interpolation of intermezzos was planned with vast scenic designs and continuous music. There were to be four, representing *Musica della terra, del mare, dell' aria* and *Musica celeste*. Typical for Vincenzo was the fact that all this vast trouble and expense was to please one of his mistresses, the Spanish beauty Agnese d'Argotti. The play was put in rehearsal and arrangements were made for a brilliant illumination of the courtyard by a thousand torches and for vast tapestries to cover the walls. Alas, the performance never came off. The official reason given was the death of Cardinal Gioanvincenzo Gonzaga in Rome; [1] more malicious tongues whispered that the true one was the disapproval of the duchess. We know that musicians were to have been brought from as far as Venice and Verona and Ferrara, and they must have spent some time in Mantua rehearsing. May not Monteverdi have been among them?

[1] *Vide* W. W. Grey, *Pastoral Poetry and Pastoral Drama* (London, 1906).

This interest in drama was enough to make Vincenzo keep an adequate musical establishment, since plays always involved music, quite apart from the intermezzos which were given between the acts, with great machines, splendid scenery, and singing and dancing. Vincenzo seems also to have been fond of music itself. Admittedly he seems to have had less perception than his father. The really famous composers of the court—Monteverdi excepted—were those left over from previous years. His performers, on the other hand, were excellent. The singers, especially, were the most famous of their age—and from all accounts such women as Adriana Basile and Caterinuccia Martinelli were superb. This was the beginning of the age of virtuosity, an age where the prestige of the princely court was felt to be more at stake in the quality of the performers than the composers.

Concerts took place every Friday in the great Hall of Mirrors ot the Gonzaga Palace—so one of Monteverdi's letters tells us; and although we have no descriptions of them, we can imagine what happened from a description of a concert at the nearby court of the Estensi at Ferrara. The two courts were very similar, and their composers often visited each other. The performers were more jealously guarded, and there was a great deal of rivalry between the two cities. Mantua could hardly compete with the grand instrumental *ensembles* of Ferrara, but the Gonzagas did everything to keep up with the standards of virtuosity set by several of the Ferrara singers. So we may take the letter of the Roman ambassador at Ferrara as giving a lively account of the sort of evening which was so popular at Mantua also:

The day before yesterday the court returned from Belriguardo, where I had stayed for two days upon the invitation of the duke. . . . In the morning we rode in a small open carriage, as is the custom, until the duchess was ready to go to Mass. After that we had dinner, and this was immediately followed by a game of cards, at which were present the duke and duchess, Lady Marfisa and I. And I cannot refrain from mentioning, since it is an inevitable custom here, that at once the music began, and I was forced to admire all the florid passages, cadences and other ornamentations: of these bagatelles, the cards included, I understand very little, and I care for them even less. These festivities lasted not one minute less than four hours, for after several ladies had sung, there finally appeared Lady Perperara—that lady from Mantua about whom I wrote before, and on the pretext that I should hear her sing now this thing, now that, both solo and accompanied, with one or more instruments, she continued to perform beyond one's endurance. . . .[1]

To come from provincial Cremona into this atmosphere of courtly service, to mix with these great singers and players, to work under a fine composer such as Wert, must have changed Monteverdi's life considerably. Certainly it changed and matured his music, for he published his third book of madrigals in 1592, and this was no work of a provincial composer. The music of the other Mantuan composers had clearly had its effect—and this more up-to-date style made Monteverdi's music more popular. The book must have paid his publisher Amadino, since it was reprinted within two years. In the dedication Monteverdi naturally offers the book to his master, Duke Vincenzo. For the most part it is written in that conventional and flowery language we meet in all dedicatory letters of the time; but there is a hint that Monteverdi regarded 'his most noble service of playing the viol', as he called it, more as a gateway into the world of the court music than as an end in itself. He was clearly hoping for the better things that befitted a composer. He was not disappointed, for the next news we have of him is that he has raised his status from player to singer; and by this time he was senior enough for his patron to take him on an expedition. Duke Vincenzo was called upon by the Emperor Rudolf to aid him in a war against the Turks. The Turks were now in possession of a great deal of south-east Europe, and were menacing Austria from Hungary. At first Vincenzo sent troops to be directly under the command of the Emperor. Shortly afterwards he decided to go himself, to be at the head of his own army. Following the custom of the day, he took a formidable retinue with him, and among them were some of his musicians.

Monteverdi was at the head of a little group of five musicians. The journey was no doubt exhausting but also beautiful: across the Alps

[1] Translation adapted from C. G. Anthon, *Music and Musicians in Northern Italy during the Sixteenth Century* (Harvard thesis, 1943), page 258.

MONTEVERDI IN MIDDLE AGE
Portrait by an unknown painter

to Innsbruck, then Prague and Vienna, before the plains of Hungary. The warlike activities were brief enough, and not particularly success-ful. After the assault of one fortress the duke returned home, having been six months away. Such an expedition would in the normal way be hardly worth mentioning; it can scarcely have added much to Monteverdi's musical experience. But it seems to have affected him deeply. He remembered it vividly nearly forty years later, and warlike scenes became one of his principal interests as an artist. It is no coin-cidence that his last book of madrigals contains *madrigali guerrieri*, nor that he chose to set the battle scenes from Tasso's *Gerusalemme liberata*.

He arrived home richer in experience but poorer in pocket. As he said in a later letter: 'If it was my good fortune that the Most Serene Duke graciously allowed me to serve him in Hungary, it was bad luck that I had additional expenditure on account of the journey from which our poor home suffers even at the present time.' [1] To make matters worse he seems to have been disappointed when, on the death of Giaches de Wert in 1596, Benedetto Pallavicino was promoted to be *maestro di cappella* to the duke. Certain biographers of Monteverdi have sought explanations for the appointment of this mediocrity, as they have called him, over the head of a genius. The truth is simple. In 1596 Monteverdi was still not thirty, and although admittedly a composer of merit had shown no signs of that overwhelming popu-larity which was to appear ten years later. Pallavicino was older, had published a great deal of music and in any case at that time was not considered a mediocrity. Two contemporary writers—Artusi and Banchieri—both had good words to say of his music, and some of it even today seems remarkably fine. So we have no need to assume any intrigues. Regarded in this light, it was merely a matter of seniority; and now Monteverdi headed the salary list of the singers at court and was next in line for promotion.

We hear nothing more of Monteverdi until 1599. Then he married a court singer, Claudia Cattaneo. It was a marriage in a modern tradition, for she presumably kept on working, as her salary was

[1] G. F. Malipiero, *Claudio Monteverdi* (Milan, 1929), page 135.

continued until her death, although she had had children. The pair were married on 20th May, but they had little time to enjoy themselves. Monteverdi again had to accompany his patron on a journey. In June 1599 Vincenzo set out for Flanders, to spend a month at the bathing resort of Spa, before visiting Liège and Antwerp, where he bought paintings and antiques, and finally Brussels. This must have been a more interesting journey to a musician. On such travels the court was not content merely to listen to its own performers. Local singers and players performed before the duke and were well rewarded for their pains. It must have been from these that Monteverdi learned 'the French style of singing' which his brother mentioned some years later in his preface to the *Scherzi musicali*. Again he returned home richer in experience and poorer in pocket:

If my good fortune called me into the service of His Highness in Flanders, on this occasion also it went against me in that Signora Claudia, remaining in Cremona, had to keep up the expenditure of our home, with maid and servant, yet had only forty-seven lire a month from His Highness, besides that which my father gave me beforehand.[1]

If Monteverdi was not happy, at least his fame was becoming more widely spread. In 1600 a theorist, Giovanni Maria Artusi, who lived in Bologna, produced a book, *L'Artusi, overo delle Imperfettioni della moderna musica*. The attack, as the title suggests, is on modern music, and although Monteverdi is nowhere mentioned by name, his works come in for the brunt of the assault. There are a number of quotations from some of his madrigals (not as yet published), all of them to show 'irregularities' of harmony or counterpoint. No one attacks mediocrities. There is no point in writing a book to criticize the work of someone completely unknown, and from the setting of the book, the private house of one of the Ferrarese gentry, we may gather that Monteverdi was a leading light of a circle of composers which included some of the most progressive of the day. For the moment this is more important news than the attack itself, for we have had no

[1] Ibid., page 136.

works from Monteverdi's pen published for eight years, and Artusi's evidence shows the way his mind was working and his standing in his middle thirties.

It is not very surprising, therefore, to find that when Pallavicino died in the following year Monteverdi applied to Duke Vincenzo for the post of *maestro di cappella*. The tone of his letter is interesting:

... if, when the world has seen my zeal in Your Highness's service and your graciousness to me after the death of the most famous Signor Striggio, and after that of the excellent Signor Giaches [de Wert], and thirdly after that of the most excellent Signor Franceschino [Rovigo] and finally after this the death of the capable Benedetto Pallavicino—if I failed to seek (on the grounds not of merit but of the faithful and singular devotion that I have always given in Your Highness's service) the ecclesiastical post now vacant, and if after all this I were not to ask with vigour and with humility for the said rank, it could be claimed with justice that I was negligent.[1]

This letter, the first we possess, is typical of Monteverdi's writing, especially when he feels strongly about something. The complete lack of punctuation (the first full stop comes nearly at the end of a very long letter) and the piling of clause upon clause gives us a vivid picture of the temper of the man. It requires little imagination to see him, now after about ten years at Mantua, rather jealous of others, conscious of every imagined slight on his worth and well aware that gossip could undermine his position. Mantua, with its enclosed atmosphere, had left its mark on Monteverdi's character. Who can wonder if he became considered a difficult man in this small community?

On this occasion, however, he had no cause to complain. He was made *maestro di cappella* with full control of both court and church music. The addition to his income must have been welcome, since he was now the father of Francesco, born in 1601. The elevation in his status, one would imagine, must have contented him for a time, for his new post was equal to any in Italy, except some in Rome or Venice. And now the tide began to turn, at least as far as his fame was

[1] Ibid., page 128.

concerned. In 1603 he published his fourth book of madrigals with his old publisher Amadino. The contents were the work of several years, as he suggests in the preface (Artusi's attack of 1600 helps in dating some of them), and his dedication is not to anyone in Mantua but to the members of the Accademia degli Intrepidi at Ferrara, whose musicians were probably more his friends than those nearer home. The book was an immediate success and went through a number of editions quite quickly. Artusi followed up with another attack, this time naming the culprit who perpetrated his crimes against the traditions of music.

Either the success of this volume, or the desire for an opportunity to reply to Artusi, made Monteverdi publish yet another collection of madrigals soon after this in 1605. Again the contents were the work of some years, and this time he wrote a preface in addition to the usual dedication:

Do not wonder that I am allowing these madrigals to be printed without first replying to the attacks which Artusi has made against certain short passages in them. Since being in the service of His Serene Highness of Mantua I have not the time which would be required to do so; I have nevertheless written a reply to make known that I do not compose haphazardly, and as soon as it is rewritten it will be published bearing the title Second Practice or On the Perfection of Modern Music, which will perhaps surprise those who do not believe that there is any other way of composition save that taught by Zarlino; but let them be assured that, with regard to consonances and dissonances, there is yet another consideration different from those usually held, which defends the modern method of composition while giving satisfaction to the reason and the senses, and this I have wished to say, so that this expression 'second practice' may not be used by anyone else and the ingenious may reflect upon other secondary matters concerning music, and believe that the modern composer builds upon the foundations of truth.

Farewell.

The book to which he refers occupied his thoughts until his last years, but it was never published. The reason was probably that he was conscious of his limitations as a writer and as a scholar. The apparatus of Greek philosophy which was expected of the writer on music was beyond him; and the fact that most of his contemporaries were equally in the dark but went on writing all the same did not encourage him.

Treatise or no treatise, this fifth volume of madrigals made Monteverdi's reputation quite secure. Not only was it reprinted within a year; his publisher found it financially expedient to reprint all his earlier books as well. But his position at Mantua was no happier than before. The irregularity in the payment of his salary was, to say the least, very trying. In a letter written in October 1604 we learn of his plight:

As a last resort it is necessary for me to have recourse to Your Highness's most infinite generosity, so that the last word can be said about that pay that was granted by Your Highness's grace. I come, however, to your feet, with as much humility as I can, to ask you to look upon my plight, not because of my boldness in writing this letter but because of the very great need about which I am writing; I do not write to the president, who many times has said yes in a most friendly and polite manner, but then, however good his intentions, has never wished to pay me except when it pleases him, so that it becomes necessary to ask him almost as though I were indebted to him and not to the generosity of Your Highness, who has been full of grace even to servants of little merit. . . . This letter of mine has no other end than to come to your feet to ask Your Highness to give the order for my pay which is now five months in arrears, in which plight is also Signora Claudia, and my father-in-law, and the sum increases in this way so that I see no hope of having it in the future without a special order from Your Highness, without which all my labours will remain failing and ruinous since day by day I am running up debts and I cannot repay them.[1]

In other words the treasurer, with whom Monteverdi has quarrelled, was holding up his pay;[2] and Monteverdi's debts were mounting,

[1] Ibid., page 129.

[2] This letter and later ones seem to suggest that it was mainly the treasurer who refused Monteverdi's pay and that the dukes of Mantua were generous enough. However, there are a number of documents in the Gonzaga archives which show the continual reluctance of the dukes to pay up. Perhaps the most pathetic is a plea from the town musicians of Mantua:

in part because Claudia was again staying in Cremona with her father-in-law, having had her third child, a son, who was born in May and called Massimiliano.[1] Monteverdi himself went to Cremona, probably to be there at his wife's confinement, and a letter written to Mantua tells us something of the work he was engaged on.

Significantly enough it was stage music. Monteverdi must have had some experience in this *genre* as a performer, for Guarini's *Il pastor fido* had not only been put into rehearsal in 1591; it was finally given a full performance in 1598. But this is the first knowledge we have of his composition for the stage, and at once we see his interest in the practical details. His commission was to write dances for what appears to have been either a pastoral play in the fashionable style of Tasso and Guarini or an intermezzo. One dance is an *entrata* for the stars, another is for shepherds, and Monteverdi says in his letter that he cannot proceed until he knows the number of dancers involved, for he would like to plan the dance with a number of *pas de deux* intermingled with a refrain for the whole *corps de ballet*. So he has already written to the dancing master and when he has the information, he will immediately set to work.

This letter is interesting, for it shows Monteverdi already fully aware of the necessity to plan the stagework and music together; and thus fascinated by the possibilities of dramatic music, he must have welcomed the opportunity to write an opera. This came when the festivities for the Carnival season of 1607 were planned. The details of

---

'A reminder to Your Highness from the players who served you at the baptism at which there were seven festivals and seven days during which they had been in the service of Your Highness of Gonzaga, begging Your Highness to give them satisfaction for

They are poor men.'

Arch. Gonzaga *Busta* 402.

[1] For details of the birth of Monteverdi's children see C. Gallico, 'Newly discovered documents concerning Monteverdi' in the *Musical Quarterly*, XLVIII (1962). Only two of the three seem to have survived beyond early childhood.

the conception and the performance of the new opera are unknown to us. The idea of producing an opera must have been in Vincenzo Gonzaga's mind for some time, since he had seen the Peri-Caccini opera *Euridice* in Florence during the wedding festivities of Maria de' Medici and Henry IV of France in 1600. Vincenzo's sons Ferdinando and Francesco were also interested in such activities, and as no doubt these were the mainstays of the Accademia degli Invaghiti, it was only a matter of time before this body decided to become a rival of the Florentine academies where opera had been born.

Monteverdi's opera was on the same subject as the Florentine opera of 1600—the story of Orpheus and Eurydice; but the work was a local production. The Mantuan court chancellor Striggio, the son of the composer whom we have already mentioned, wrote the libretto. The Mantuan virtuosos were probably given the principal parts, although we know that at least one singer was brought from Florence. The first performance took place before the members of the academy (probably in the Palazzo Ducale);[1] and then the opera was given more performances in front of the court with its guests. The libretto was published for the occasion, the score of the opera two years later. No description of the production exists, but we can assume that, if it resembled other such entertainments for the Carnival, it was a sumptuous one. In any case it was a great success, so much so that the Mantuan court must have looked forward to another opportunity for opera in the following year.

Professionally, *Orfeo* was a triumph, yet Monteverdi had little chance to enjoy it. His wife had been ill since at least November 1606, which was worrying enough in itself, and worrying because, as Claudia herself wrote: 'My serious illness has made me spend money which I cannot afford.' In July of the following year we find Monteverdi in Cremona, where Claudia could be looked after by his father. Work still followed him there and the duke was wanting more music

---

[1] There seems to be no reason to assume, with H. F. Redlich, that it took place in the state rooms of the academy—if they had them. 'In the academy', the phrase on the title-page of the libretto, surely means 'in front of the members of the academy'.

from him. Monteverdi could only reply that he was doing his best but he was tired and unwell. In August some of his music was performed before the Cremonese Accademia degli Animosi, and the academy made him an honorary member. Later in the month he went to Milan to show one of his oldest friends the score of *Orfeo*. At about the same time his *Scherzi musicali* were published in Venice with a new reply to Artusi, this time (and understandably in the circumstances) written by his brother.

In spite of all these successes, the honour in his home town, the popularity of the new book, the praise of his Milanese friend and the publication of yet another book of madrigals (old ones turned into *madrigali spirituali* by another friend living in Milan), personal tragedy was overwhelming. Claudia Monteverdi died on 10th September and was buried at Cremona. Monteverdi was at this time forty years of age, and he had been married for eight of them. His surviving children were aged six and three. It is no wonder he was in despair. Ironically, now was the least convenient time to give way to it. Duke Vincenzo's eldest son, heir to the throne, was to marry Margherita of Savoy. The celebrations were to include as many magnificent *spettacoli* as possible, including a new opera by Monteverdi.

He had the desire neither to resume work nor to return to Mantua. Why should he return to where the envy of colleagues and the lack of appreciation of his talents had made his life a misery, and everything about him must remind him of Claudia? Only a letter from his friend Follino, court chronicler, could make him consent to leave his father's house at Cremona:

SIGNOR CLAUDIO,

I do not know how to dissemble nor am I a flatterer, so please believe me that I have seen in the eyes of the prince and I have heard from his voice such things in praise of your genius that I have good, even excellent hopes for you; I believe that in the past you have known me to be affectionate, even most affectionate to my friends, and in particular to you yourself in such matters; so accept my advice, which is to forget now all these troubles, to return here and quickly, since this is the time to acquire the greatest fame which a man may have on earth and all the gratitude of the Most Serene Prince.[1]

Monteverdi returned to Mantua to try to submerge his sorrows in work.

There was plenty of this. The entry of Francesco and his bride into Mantua after their wedding in Turin was to mark the beginning of a week of dramatic entertainment, which for splendour and expense even in its own day was exceptional. Royal weddings had to be accompanied by such costly rejoicing, for these were the occasions when the succession was assured (or at least so it was hoped). Elegant and prosperous festivity was reassuring to all parties, quite apart from providing the occasion for hero worship on the part of the lower orders. Given this custom and the newness of Mantua's discovery of opera, we can understand how the celebrations of 1608 took shape. There was to be the usual play—Guarini's *Idropica*—with intermezzos; a triumph or masque by the bridegroom himself, two ballets—one of them in the opulent French style—and of course the new opera. No expense was to be spared. Naturally some singers would have to come from elsewhere—from Florence. When it became evident that Monteverdi and the other Mantuans could hardly be expected to compose everything, another Florentine, Marco da Gagliano, was commissioned to write one of the ballets and an intermezzo to *Idropica*. Yet one more Florentine was involved, the poet Rinuccini, who had supplied the book for the earlier operas produced in Florence and who was now to write the libretti for the new opera and one of the ballets.

Monteverdi's share of the work was enormous. The new opera *Arianna* was his; so was the music for one of the intermezzos and one of the ballets. This was a staggering task, the more so since the wedding seemed likely to take place early in the new year, and the music had to be composed and rehearsed by the Carnival season. Monteverdi arrived back in Mantua early in October. On 9th October he had no libretto

[1] S. Davari, *Notizie biografiche del distinto maestro di musica Claudio Monteverdi* (Mantua, 1885), page 12.

and obviously felt the pressure of time, since Prince Francesco wrote to his father:

> Yesterday evening Monteverdi came to speak with me, and showing his desire to serve Your Highness well in the wedding festivities and especially in the pastoral play which is to be set to music, he insisted that should you wish him to write it, it would be necessary for him to have the words in the next seven or eight days so that he could begin to work, since otherwise it will not be enough for his spirit to do good work in the short time between now and Carnival.[1]

We know from other letters that Monteverdi was not a quick composer, and to have under four months to produce a complete opera, a *genre* in which he had had little practice, was nearly impossible. In November Ferdinando, Francesco's brother, was taking precautions to see that there would be an opera during Carnival, even if it was not Monteverdi's, and had written to Florence for Gagliano, who came to Mantua with the score of his *Dafne* (already composed though not as yet produced). This was put into rehearsal and performed in January. Nevertheless, Monteverdi had not failed his master. By the beginning of February *Arianna* was almost finished.

At this point there was a new disaster. The prima donna who was to sing the title role fell ill with smallpox. This was a severe blow for Monteverdi. It came so suddenly (the singer had taken part in *Dafne* a week or two earlier) that it completely disrupted the production of *Arianna*. More than that, Caterinuccia Martinelli was one of Monteverdi's closest friends. She had been brought to Mantua from Rome in 1603, aged thirteen. The possessor of a particularly fine voice, she was the pride of the court and had lodged with Monteverdi since her arrival. Although, as it happened, she did not 'create' the role of Arianna, it was certainly created for her, and her illness was the worst thing which could have happened at this time. At first it looked hopeless, then she improved; finally she died, after being ill for over a month.

[1] De' Paoli, *Claudio Monteverdi* (Milan, 1945), page 127.

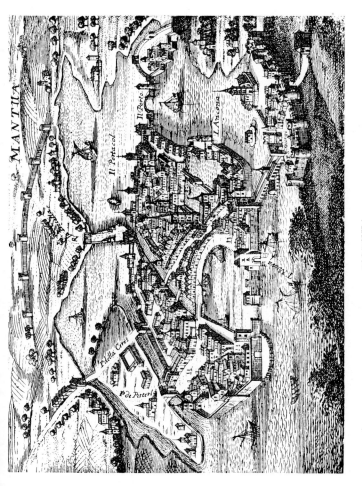

MANTUA

From a seventeenth-century engraving

By this time Carnival was over, but fortunately all was not lost. The ceremonial entry into Mantua had been put back into the spring, and the best thing to do was to postpone the performance of *Arianna* until the main marriage celebrations at the end of May. The first idea for a new singer was the daughter of Caccini, but she was singing another part and this would have meant two changes in the cast. Monteverdi then suggested a singer from Bergamo, who, however, would not come. Then someone had the brilliant idea of asking one of the actresses from the cast of *Idropica*. She turned out to be suitable and rehearsals went ahead. In the meantime, Monteverdi had still to write the music for one intermezzo and compose a long ballet, *Il ballo delle ingrate*.

The prince and his new wife arrived from Turin on 24th May with a train of guests from all over Italy. Four days later *Arianna* was given. There were some four thousand people—only a few of them from Mantua—packing the court theatre, and their enthusiasm is described by Follino in rapturous terms:

This work was very beautiful in itself both because of the people who took part, dressed in clothes no less appropriate than splendid, and for the scenery, which represented a wild rocky place in the midst of the waves, which in the furthest part of the prospect could be seen always in motion, giving a charming effect. But since to this was joined the force of the music by Signor Claudio Monteverdi, *maestro di cappella* to the duke, a man whose worth is known to all the world, and who in this work excelled himself, combining with the union of the voices a harmony of the instruments disposed behind the scene which always accompanied the voices, and as the mood of the music changed, so was the sound of the instruments varied; and seeing that it was acted by men and women who were all excellent singers, every part succeeded well, most especially miraculously in the lament which Ariadne sings on the rock when she has been abandoned by Theseus, which was acted with much emotion and in so piteous a way that no one hearing it was left unmoved, nor among the ladies was there one who did not shed a few tears at her plaint.[1]

As we have seen, Follino was a close friend of the composer, and

[1] De' Paoli, op. cit., page 139.

anyway, as court chronicler his account of *Arianna* would have had to record a great success. But there are many ways in which we can confirm his judgment. Time after time there are passages in Monteverdi's letters which refer to the power of the opera. The theorist Doni knew the score of at least the lament about 1640, a long time for any music to be remembered in the seventeenth century; nor must we forget that the opera was revived at least twice in the next thirty years, again unusual for a work which was written specially and hurriedly for a great occasion. As for the lament which Follino praised so lavishly, imitation certainly proved the sincerest form of flattery, for laments became the stock-in-trade of composers for half a century. They appeared not only in operas but also in the song-books and madrigal-books, written by bad, mediocre and good composers. Monteverdi himself was able to make money from his lament and published arrangements of it. In fact, the 'Lament of Ariadne' was the first great popular operatic *scena*.

After *Arianna* the music for the prologue for *Idropica*, and even *Il ballo delle ingrate*, must have seemed less important. The intermezzo was as ephemeral as most of these productions, and the music has disappeared. The ballet has survived, for later in life Monteverdi included it in his last book of madrigals. It is an important work, and clearly in its staging made a great effect, yet the music shows signs of the haste with which Monteverdi wrote it, and it remains little to console us for the loss of *Arianna*, the score of which has not yet been discovered.

'The greatest fame which a man may have on earth and all the gratitude of the Most Serene Prince'—these were Follino's inducements to return to Mantua. Both were Monteverdi's in June 1608. Neither could alleviate his misery. He returned to Cremona in a state of complete collapse. In November his father was desperate enough to write to the Duchess of Mantua to ask if Claudio could be released from his duties:

If he returns to Mantua the heavy duties and the unhealthy air will soon result in his death, and the burden of his two children will come upon me, which would be terrible on account of both my age and lack of money, since I have had to support his wife and others on behalf of the said Claudio when he went with His Highness to Hungary and Flanders and also when he came to Cremona with his wife, servants, carriage and children.[1]

If his father was worried by the prospect of his return to the court, Monteverdi himself was furious, and when a letter came on the last day of November, bidding him return, he replied at great length and with considerable heat. What has he ever gained from Mantua except hard work and debts, he asks. What has he gained from his splendid success at the recent wedding festivities? All that has happened is that his wife's salary has been stopped, and even the pension of a hundred scudi which the duke had promised him has turned out to be only seventy. No other Mantuan musician has had such bad treatment and certainly no foreigner. Bitterly he asks the court chancellor:

Do you wish, Your Excellency, for anything to be clearer; to give two hundred scudi to M. Marco da Gagliano who could be said to have done nothing new, and to me, who did all that I did, nothing at all? Knowing this, how ill and unfortunate I am in Mantua, I ask you, Most Excellent Sig. Chieppo, for the love of God, to help me to have permission to leave from His Highness, for I know that from this alone can come my well-being. Signor Federico Follino promised me in his letter asking me to return to Mantua from Cremona for work on the marriage celebrations, he promised me, I say, that which Your Excellency can see in this letter of his which I am sending, and yet in the end nothing has been done, and all that I have had is one thousand five hundred lines to set to music.[2]

Monteverdi was not accorded permission to leave. Instead his pay was raised to three hundred scudi a year, and his pension, 'for himself, his heir, and successors of any kind . . . of a hundred scudi each worth six lire of our Mantuan money', was formally granted to him.

When he actually returned to the court is unknown. His two surviving letters of 1609 were written from Cremona, but as they date

---

[1] De' Paoli, op. cit., page 150.
[2] Malipiero, op. cit., page 138.

from August and September it is possible that he had gone back to his father for the summer, after working again during the Carnival season. These letters and others in the next two years show us that the worst of his depression had passed by now. In 1610 he was working on a book of madrigals, including an arrangement for five voices of 'Ariadne's Lament' and another lament in commemoration of Caterinuccia Martinelli. Later in the same year he went to Rome to see if he could find a publisher for some church music which he intended to dedicate to the Pope, and also to try to obtain a scholarship to the Papal Seminary for his son Francesco. He could count on the influence of Ferdinando Gonzaga, now a cardinal, to whom Vincenzo's heir, Francesco, wrote in advance on behalf of the composer. Nothing came of either venture. The church music was printed by his Venetian publisher. His son was not given his bursary.

Was Monteverdi seeking a new post at this time? It seems quite likely. For a man not much given to travelling about, his Roman journey and one to Venice which followed immediately were unusual. Even less usual was his new interest in church music. We do not possess a note of his church music (as distinct from *madrigali spirituali*) before 1610. Then we find him writing a Mass in the Roman *a cappella* style, a Mass which cost him a great deal of study and hard work. We also have a letter which tells us that Monteverdi presented the duke with a *Dixit* for five voices and also a little motet for two voices to be sung at the Elevation and another for five voices in honour of the Blessed Virgin for Easter 1610. It is possible that the departure of Gastoldi—the official *maestro di cappella* of the ducal chapel of S. Barbara—to a post in Milan had caused this new activity. But it can scarcely be a coincidence that the principal posts in Venice and Rome demanded a knowledge of church music.

For Monteverdi was now at a difficult stage. He was so distinguished that, if he wished to move, posts which would be suitable for him were rare. As a court musician his chances were meagre. The court of the Estensi was now much reduced, following the secession of Ferrara and its province to the papal dominions on the death of Duke Alfonso. Parma, Turin and Milan were far less interested in music. Florence had its own composers. To accept an ordinary post as *maestro di cappella* at a cathedral was to retreat in social and financial status. Only St Mark's in Venice and the larger churches in Rome were of the right dignity for such a distinguished composer. The matter became more urgent in 1612. Vincenzo Gonzaga died. His son Francesco ascended the throne, and Monteverdi might well have been pleased about this, for Francesco had been especially keen on operatic entertainments. But some time in July he suddenly dismissed both Monteverdi and his brother Giulio Cesare. No reason is given in the documents. Perhaps it was something to do with the usual festival which was mounted on these occasions. There was certainly a public festival on 25th July to celebrate the election of a relative of Francesco Gonzaga as Holy Roman Emperor. The duke himself wrote a *torneo*, depicting the Rape of the Sabines; there were fireworks, and on the following Sunday some splendid music in S. Barbara.[1] Was Monteverdi ordered to write the music for church or *torneo*? If so, it would have had to be done at short notice, something which he always detested. He may well have refused to fall in with the duke's plans. In any case he left Mantua for good with just twenty-five scudi in his pocket as his savings after over twenty years in the service there.

He returned to Cremona, and having nothing to do, went to Milan in September, probably to visit his many friends there. Malicious tongues said that he was intriguing for the post of *maestro di cappella* of Milan Cathedral over the head of the incumbent, who was pleasing the authorities there well enough. This story was not true, as the Mantuan ambassador in Milan reported after making inquiries. After this we have no news of the composer for nearly a year. Then his luck changed. The *maestro di cappella* at St Mark's in Venice died in July 1613. The procurators of St Mark's, instead of merely advertising the post in Venice and its subject cities on the mainland, decided to make a wider search for a suitably distinguished musician, and wrote to the ambassadors and residents in Rome, Padua, Vicenza, Brescia, Bergamo, Milan and Mantua. The letter to Milan (for Cremona was

[1] Arch. Ven., *Dispacci, Senato III (Secreta), Mantova, Filza* 1 b, fo. 29.

in its province) shows clearly that they already had Monteverdi in mind:

On the death of the Most Reverend *maestro di cappella* of our church of St Mark there have been several people proposed, among whom is Signor Claudio Monteverdi, *maestro di cappella* to His Highness. We should there-fore be very happy to have a report informing us of his worth and efficiency, and if you think of any other person we should be in your debt in having news about him.[1]

This letter left Venice on 16th July. The procurators must have received a favourable reply, for by 19th August Monteverdi was in Venice rehearsing some church music with the players and singers of St Mark's. The rehearsal took place in the church of S. Giorgio, after which the music was given in the basilica itself. It was a sumptuous work which needed twenty players and two portable organs in addition to the thirty or so salaried musicians; and it pleased the procurators. They appointed Monteverdi on the spot and gave him fifty ducats to show him how they did business.[2] Monteverdi went back home to Cremona to make arrangements for removing to Venice. On his way to take up his new appointment he had his last disaster. He was robbed by highwaymen and lost all his money. Then he crossed the lagoon to the city which was to be his final resting-place. Thereafter, in so far as he was capable of happiness, he was a happy man. Fame, prosperity and the better health which contentment often gives were to be his in the Most Serene Republic.

[1] Arch. Ven., *Proc. de Supra, Reg.* 193*bis*, fo. 64. See Appendix E (page 202).

[2] Arch. Ven., *Proc. de Supra, Cassier, Chiesa, Reg.* 10, 22nd Aug. 1613.

CHAPTER III

VENICE

THE procurators of St Mark's had made their choice with great speed. Usually they took their time in choosing a new *maestro di cappella*, with an interregnum of six months or more. They must have had unusual confidence in Monteverdi's reputation and demeanour. He was old enough, had experience in administration and was a famous composer. Someone of this stature was very necessary, since Monteverdi's predecessor had been a failure. Giulio Cesare Martinengo had come to St Mark's from Udine Cathedral. He left no mark on history as a composer, and worse still, he seems to have had unsatisfactory dealings with the procurators. The account books of the basilica show that he was constantly in debt almost from the moment he set foot in Venice. To pay his creditors he was continually asking for advances on his pay, and eventually died owing the treasurer several months' salary. To hasten the decline of Venetian music still further, the last of the great older school of composers, Giovanni Gabrieli, had died the year before Monteverdi's arrival. Given these circumstances, we can understand their welcome of an acknowledged master.

Monteverdi's new post was an onerous one. The musical establishment of St Mark's was large, perhaps the largest in Italy. There were about thirty singers, some of them *castrati*, and six players in regular employment, besides the boys of the choir school. In addition, on festival days it was usual to hire about fifteen extra instrumentalists, and to pay them *per diem*. There were two excellent organists, often composers of merit themselves, and a vice-*maestro*, usually a promoted singer, who helped to maintain discipline, and took on his shoulders the burden of teaching the boys and the younger priests the arts of plainsong and counterpoint. The minutes of the procurators' meetings show how much administration was involved in keeping the *cappella* routine in order. New singers to be tested and hired, music to be composed and copied, the players to be hired—all these and many other duties must have kept Monteverdi busy.

For a *maestro* like Monteverdi, appointed mainly on his reputation as a composer, the frequency of the Venetian festivals must have presented many problems. There were about forty festivals, all of them celebrated with the greatest pomp and involving music. These were days which we can relive today only at coronations, royal weddings, jubilees and the like. A great procession would form in the Doge's Palace—the clergy in their robes, the ambassadors and papal nuncio in their most brilliant regalia, the Doge and Senate in their brightly coloured gowns—and then would go round the great square to enter St Mark's by its west door. There Mass and vespers were sung and played, and the procession would retreat in all its glory. The whole populace would also be there, staring from the porticoes in the square, leaning out of their windows, even climbing on the roofs of the Procuratoria if they could find a way up. On Ascension Day the ceremonies were made even more picturesque by the use of the *Bucintoro*, the Doge's barge, which took the Doge and the Senate to a place near the Lido, where the Doge threw a ring into the sea, to 'wed' Venice to its mistress, the cause of its prosperity and glory.

This was all very well for the splendour-loving Venetian, but for the composer it meant a hardworking life from which there was no escape. For one thing, the liturgy used in St Mark's was unique, and therefore some of the motet texts were set only by Venetian composers. For another, the magnificence of the music required meant that the Masses and vesper psalms of composers outside Venice were rarely on a large enough scale. Sometimes works by recently deceased Venetians such as Croce and the Gabrielis were used, but new music was always needed. For Monteverdi it can scarcely have been easy, since there was no other composer in St Mark's in his first few years, nor had his duties in Mantua really prepared him for the rapid composition of church music. So his letters to Striggio at Mantua often have to apologize for a delay due to lack of time. In February 1615 he is sorry that he cannot leave Venice to fulfil a commission from the duke since 'I must serve in St Mark's, because of the approach of Holy Week, at which time take place many functions attended by The Most Serene Signory [i.e. the Senate]'.[1] Four years later he was unable to compose a madrigal or cantata of some kind 'on account of the affairs of Holy Week that will occupy me at St Mark's, and the festivals, which are of no little importance to the *maestro di cappella*'.[2]

Yet it would be a mistake to interpret these as complaints, or even as meaning that he felt he was wasting time when he could have been writing opera. Certainly there was a great change in Monteverdi himself. From the tired, depressed, ageing man he seemed in the later years at Mantua he became a renewed, invigorated and thoroughly alive composer and *maestro*. The amount of work he did in his first few years at Venice was enormous. The Acts of the Procurators show that he thoroughly reorganized the *cappella*. He gradually brought the choir up to strength, hired more virtuoso *castrati*, and made them all work harder. Whereas in former years singers were needed only for the greater festivals (indeed this fact was used to attract good foreigners), Monteverdi insisted on sung Masses on the ferial days. He found that there was little music available for the choir, and persuaded the procurators to buy some part-books from the Gardano press, to build up a repertory of *a cappella* music by Palestrina, Soriano, Lambardi and others. He also regularized the position of the instrumentalists. Instead of paying the majority on a daily basis as they were required, he arranged to have them placed on the salary roll of the treasurer, so that they were paid bi-monthly, as were the rest of the staff of St Mark's.[3]

In spite of this he found enough time to compose and publish secular music. The contents of his sixth book of madrigals were certainly written at Mantua, but he saw the book through the press only in 1614, putting his proud new title on the front page. Then there were commissions from Mantua (now rapidly going downhill as a

---

[1] Malipiero, op. cit., page 157.
[2] Ibid., page 181.
[3] Arch. Ven., *Proc. de Supra, Chiesa Actorum* 135, fo. 9.

musical centre and having no composer of distinction any longer), including a ballet *Tirsi e Clori*, which was composed in 1615, and what amounts to an opera, commissioned in the following year. The latter, a *favola marittima* called *Le nozze de Tetide*, caused him a good deal of trouble before he finally abandoned it in January 1617. He seems to have spent over a month trying to make the libretto into something suitable, and perhaps had even composed parts of it by the time he gave it up. He also seems to have fitted into the literary circles of Venice quite happily. He sent a copy of his sixth book of madrigals to a minor poet, the Abbot Angelo Grillo, whom he had known a little in his Mantuan days. Grillo wrote back thanking him and referring to some manuscript works,

. . . in which you prove yourself such a great master, though you are given less support by the text; but even a mule looks like Bucephalus under a heroic rider. You have bestowed too much honour on my poems by your praise and by your music. Where my lines sound worst, there is the sweetest harmony in your composition.[1]

The procurators appreciated his hard work, and after three years we find a tangible expression of their approval in their minutes:

The procurators, knowing the worth and efficiency of D. Claudio Monteverdi, *maestro di cappella* of St Mark's, and wishing to confirm his appointment and give him the incentive to attend to the service of the Church to the honour of God with a whole heart, and in the desire that he will live and die in this service, have, by ballot, determined that he shall be confirmed in his post for ten years with a salary of 400 ducats per year with the usual perquisites.[2]

By this time he had settled the main problems in restoring the music of St Mark's, and had managed to tempt a most promising composer into Venetian service. This was Alessandro Grandi, *maestro di*

[1] A. Einstein, *Essays on Music* (1958), page 177.
[2] De' Paoli, op. cit., page 209.

L'Altra Porte della PIAZZA DI S. MARCO in Venetia.

ST MARK'S, VENICE

From a seventeenth-century engraving

cappella at Ferrara Cathedral, who was willing to enter St Mark's even as a singer. He was soon promoted, first to teach the boys in the choir school, then to be Monteverdi's deputy. Grandi must have been a great help, since he was a prolific composer with considerable experience in writing modern church music.

Monteverdi certainly needed another composer in the *cappella* during these years, since the ceremonial life of the Venetian Republic became as brilliant as it had ever been. In 1617 one of the most splendid of their processions took place, and it is worth while describing it in some detail, since it gives a fascinating idea of the atmosphere in which Monteverdi worked. During April workmen repairing the founda-tions of St Mark's found a casket with some relics in it. There was an investigation by the ecclesiastical authorities and one relic was declared to be part of the True Cross and to be stained with the blood of Christ. Such a discovery could not go by without a Mass of conse-cration and a procession, and the Master of Ceremonial in St Mark's, Cesare Vergaro, persuaded the Senate to provide money to meet the necessary expenditure. The preparations involved an incredible amount of work. New robes were made for the priests; new gloves for the people to carry the relics; the biers on which the relics were to be placed were made and covered with various rich stuffs; there was to be a new canopy for the relics. St Mark's Square was decorated by draping cloths from the windows of the Procuratoria, and carpets were hired to afford a dignified entry into the basilica.[1] Inside St Mark's a large platform (called 'a theatre' in the descriptions) was built into the middle of the choir, since it was here that the relics were to be exposed to view for three days. Four hundred copies of a booklet by Vergaro were printed and given to the nobility to explain how the relics were found and their significance. Hundreds of candles were made, and extra priests were invited to take part and were paid for the rehearsals of the ceremony.

On Sunday, 28th May, the procession took place. The relics were mounted on three biers, and the nobility came out of St Mark's to

[1] Arch. Ven., *Proc. de Supra, Cassier Chiesa, Reg.* 11.

hear an oration by the dean. Then, says Vergaro, 'there was sung the Mass of the Passion of Our Lord with most exquisite music, at the end of which a procession was formed which, passing in front of the high altar and in front of the Doge and Senate, went round the square'. After this procession the Schools, or religious confraternities, formed their own processions, each with a number of players and singers to precede the priests and brothers. Some of them had dressed floats, and the School of the Misericordia had one in which 'there was a most beautiful youth, dressed to represent the Virgin Mary'. Then came the brothers and monks from each order that had a foundation in Venice, and some of these had decorated floats too. After them came the main procession with the Doge and Senate and the relics, 'preceded by four singers who sang the Litany of the Saints, and after the relics and immediately before the Doge there was the whole body of musicians with their *maestro di cappella*'.[1]

The procession lasted an hour, and there were halts at three places in the square to adore the relics, with suitable music each time, after which the procession returned to St Mark's, where the relics were placed ceremonially on the newly erected platform. This was six feet high with steps up to it made of stone from Verona. In the middle of it was an altar on which the relics were to rest, while orations were given by various notable clerics.

> The singers retired to two platforms, one between the two large pillars . . . near the altar, the other directly opposite, singing divine praise. There was also singing from the theatre [the big platform] by a boy clad as an angel.[2]

On succeeding days there was music to accompany the exposition of the relics, and harp players were given a fee for performing this. The cost of the whole affair was about 800 ducats, an enormous sum.

What exactly Monteverdi had to do is not stated; but since in the following year he described his duties for a similar festival, we can

[1] G. C. Vergaro, *Racconto dell' apparato et solennità fatta nella Ducal Chiesa* (Venice, 1617).
[2] Ibid.

imagine his heavy burden. He writes to Striggio explaining why he cannot promise to send more of his opera *Andromeda*:

Next Thursday will be the festival of the Holy Cross . . . and it will be my duty to prepare a *messa concertata* and motets for the whole day, since the Holy Blood will be exposed on that day on an altar erected high in the middle of St Mark's, after which I must put in order [compose or rehearse?] a certain cantata in praise of His Highness, which they sing every year in the *Bucintoro* when he goes with all the Signory to marry the sea on Ascension Day, and also put in order a Mass and solemn vespers that they sing in St Mark's at that time.[1]

Hard work though it was, Monteverdi was happy. He was financially comfortable, he was famous, he was appreciated both by his employers and by the musical public at large. When an offer came from Striggio to go back (on presumably rather better terms than before) to his old job at Mantua, he contemptuously refused:

Your Highness must take into consideration how this Most Serene Republic, which never gave more than 200 ducats in salary to any of my predecessors, whether Adriano [Willaert], Cipriano [de Rore] or Zarlino, or anyone else, gives me 400 ducats, a favour which I must not lightly set aside without due consideration: since (Your Highness) this most Serene Signory never makes an innovation without due thought, I must regard this particular act of grace most favourably. Nor after this have they ever repented but have honoured me also in such a way that in the *cappella* they do not accept any report on a singer except that of the *maestro di cappella*; neither do they accept either organists or vice-*maestro* unless they have a report and opinion from the said *maestro di cappella*: there is no gentleman who does not esteem and honour me, and when I go to make either church or chamber music, I can assure Your Excellency, that the whole city runs to hear. And then my service is the more sweet since all the *cappella* is under temporal appointment except the *maestro di cappella*: on the contrary it is up to him to appoint and dismiss the singers, to grant leave of absence or not; and if he does not wish to go into the chapel, no one will say anything to him; and his position is certain until he dies, and is not made different by the death of

[1] Malipiero, op. cit., page 177.

the procurators or of the prince provided that he gives faithful and reverent service; and his salary, if he does not go to collect it at the right time, is sent to his house, and this is only his basic income. Then there is some extra money which I obtain from outside St Mark's, amounting to 200 ducats a year, having been begged and begged again by the wardens of the Schools, since anyone who wishes to have the *maestro di cappella* to make music for him must pay 30, 40 and up to 50 ducats for two vespers and a Mass, and is glad to have his service and thank him very heartily afterwards.[1]

How different it had been at Mantua, Monteverdi goes on angrily. There, the death of a prince or a change in his favour could make a very real difference. There the *maestro di cappella* was treated with no more respect than a favoured singer, either financially or otherwise. Nor had his pay even been very regular when he had had

. . . to go to the treasurer every day to beg him for what was mine by right. As God sees me, I have never in all my life felt a deeper abasement of the spirit than when it was necessary (almost for the love of God) to beg the treasurer for what was mine.

Was it really so bad at Mantua, we are tempted to ask. Were all these slights real or were they imaginary, at least in part? Surely it was not all so depressing there? But what is important is that after the small court atmosphere the change to Venice must have seemed like heaven to Monteverdi. It was a change from a dying civilization to one capable of new life.

New life is to be found everywhere in the musical activity around Monteverdi. In secular music the popular song-books by Florentine and Roman composers give way to the lively new ariettas of the Venetians. The Vincenti catalogues now contain works not only by Monteverdi and Grandi but also by lesser known composers such as Pesenti, Rovetta and Berti, all of whom were part of the Venetian musical scene. When one of the *castrati* of St Mark's, Leonardo Simonetti, made an anthology of solo motets in 1625, he could include

[1] Malipiero, op. cit., page 198.

works by no fewer than fifteen composers, all living in or around Venice. Six of them were in the employ of the basilica itself. Nor are these pieces perfunctory make-weights; they are written most competently in the latest style.

The manner and quality of the music at St Mark's in the early 1620's are described by Giulio Strozzi in a small pamphlet in which he tells of the memorial service for the late Duke of Tuscany in 1621. The Florentines living in Venice commissioned the music, which was performed in the great church of SS. Giovanni e Paolo on 25th May of that year:

> The music of the Mass and the responsories was composed and performed for the occasion by Claudio Monteverdi, whose fame makes the fine quality of the work easily understandable. In these compositions he has given expression to a particular emotion, which in transporting our princes with delight makes them honour him for his genius. The ceremonies began with a plaintive sinfonia which brought tears to the eyes, imitating the ancient Mixolydian mode rediscovered by Sappho. After the sinfonia Don Francesco Monteverdi, son of Claudio, sang with the sweetest voice the words *O vos omnes attendite*. . . . The *Dies irae* and the delicate *De profundis* were also composed by Claudio, the latter, as it were, a dialogue between souls in purgatory and angels visiting them.[1]

Unhappily, Monteverdi's music and that of his colleagues has been lost, but even the description is invaluable to us since it shows us the way his mind was working. One thing we notice is that his church music is as modern as ever—apparently a dialogue in the dramatic manner. Yet more significant is the mention of the ancients, which suggests that Monteverdi is still under the spell of the academies. This is quite remarkable, for Venice had never been a centre of academies, at least not those of the kind found at Mantua, Ferrara and Florence. Nor were his younger pupils really interested in interpreting Plato and Aristotle; and even in other centres the composers of opera and monodic madrigals and songs had turned away from these now old-fashioned ideas. This description of his requiem music shows as ever

---

[1] De' Paoli, op. cit., page 241.

the mixture of the modern and old-fashioned in Monteverdi's music, possible now only for a man of increasing middle age.

Another fruit of his fifty-odd years is the veneration which was accorded to him abroad. In 1620 he visited Bologna to settle his son Francesco's future. After a little time studying law at Bologna Francesco had decided to enter the order of Carmelite friars and came back from Bologna to Venice. There his voice was enough to procure him a post as singer in St Mark's. He had sung in the basilica as early as 1615, and the account books record a payment on 22nd April 'to Signor Claudio, *maestro di cappella*, fifty ducats of gold, and ten ducats of gold to Francesco his son for having lent his services on the days of Holy Week and Easter'.[1] Francesco had received a further payment from the procurators in 1618: '15th March: ten ducats paid to Francesco Monteverde, son of the *maestro di cappella*, for having sung the lesson at matins on last Christmas Eve.' His permanent appointment as singer took place in the 1620's and he eventually earned eighty ducats a year, which denotes that he was one of the better singers. But to settle all this in 1620 meant a journey to Bologna. Banchieri, the doyen of the Bolognese musicians, remembered several years later how 'on the day of St Anthony in the year 1620 your eminence honoured us with your presence: attending the meeting of the Florid Academy of S. Michele in Bosco'.[2] Perhaps while Monteverdi was there he discussed his other son's future, for in the following year he made arrangements for Massimiliano to study medicine at Bologna University, carefully writing to the Duchess of Mantua to use her influence with Cardinal Montalto to obtain a place in the Cardinal's College, where Massimiliano would live free from the dangers of bad company and the traditional licentiousness of Bolognese student life.

With his sons' education well organized, and the music of St Mark's running smoothly, Monteverdi was free to follow his outside interests. As he was now at the home of music-publishing we find him

[1] Arch. Ven., *Proc. de Supra, Cassier Chiesa, Reg.* 11.
[2] *Lettere armoniche* (Bologna, 1628).

writing motets for the various anthologies of church music which were so popular. His greatest music for St Mark's was composed for large resources and was not readily saleable; he therefore composed solo motets, duets and other works which could be performed more easily. Another source of income was directing the music at the school of San Rocco, which he did on the day of its patron saint in 1623 and 1628. The accounts of the school tell us that he was paid 620 lire in 1623—a huge sum—but out of this he must have had to pay the other musicians from St Mark's. More revealing is the payment for the second year, when he received a personal fee of 146 lire, or just about the amount shared among the sixteen singers of St Mark's and nearly four times the fee of even the most treasured virtuoso singer.[1]

All this activity as a composer of religious music was counter-balanced by the composition of dramatic works. Monteverdi continued his relationship with the Mantuan court. The *favola marittima* had proved no stimulus to his imagination; in its place his friend Striggio suggested another subject, Alceste. This was to be a true opera, sung throughout. The only trouble was that he had no libretto early in January 1617, and had only until Easter to complete it. The composer was keen enough to go on with the idea and even obtained leave of absence from Venice to go to Mantua for a fortnight; but even as he made his preparations a letter came cancelling the whole affair. In the autumn of the same year a commission came from Parma to compose an intermezzo to words by the duchess. We do not know whether anything came of this, either, but the project again shows the composer's reputation and the interest which others took in him.

The next libretto sent him from Mantua was *Andromeda* by Ercole Marigliani. It arrived early in 1618, and quite obviously the idea was to produce it at some time during that year. This was highly optimistic, and from the letters between Monteverdi and Striggio we can gain some idea of why the relationships at the Mantuan court had been strained during the opera festival of 1608. Monteverdi was a slow

[1] See Appendix E (page 202).

composer, especially of a large-scale work. His first letter to Mantua, after apologizing for delay because of his daily work in St Mark's, shows clearly that he is thinking of the practical details—how many women singers he can count on for the chorus and who is going to sing the part of the nuncio, since he must think about how best to write for his voice? These questions suggest that Monteverdi is about to begin composition in earnest.

Alas, the next letter, two months later, is full of apologies. The main festivals have gone, so his work in St Mark's is no excuse. This time he has been suffering 'a little from headaches caused by the heat which suddenly followed the rains', which caused him to lack ideas, and he refuses to send quick but mediocre work rather than good music a little later. In any case he has finished some pieces—a chorus of fishermen, for instance—and has planned huge sections. Then there is a large gap. More apologies follow in March 1619, when he has had the libretto for over a year; more apologies still in December. Finally, when pressed to finish the work in time for a performance during the Carnival of 1620, he writes:

I should have sent the enclosed music to Your Excellency with the last mails but Signor Marigliani at the instance of Signor D. Vincenzo asked urgently in a letter addressed to me to finish the play *Andromeda* of the said Sig. Marigliani which I had begun already, so that it could be presented before His Highness during the coming Carnival on his return from Casale. But just as I shall be forced to write it badly in order to finish it in a hurry, so I am convinced that it will be badly acted and badly played on account of the very short time, and I wonder how Sig. Marigliani is willing to commit himself to such a dubious enterprise. For there would not have been time enough if they had started rehearsing—not to mention learning—the piece before Christmas. Now what does Your Highness think it possible to do, since there are still more than four hundred lines of verse to set to music? I cannot imagine any other end than bad acting, bad playing and a bad musical *ensemble*. These are not things which can be done in such a hurry—remember *Arianna*, where it was necessary to have five months of strenuous rehearsal after they had learned their parts perfectly by heart.[1]

[1] Malipiero, op. cit., page 185.

No wonder he was considered difficult! Even if he had found the libretto to be not to his taste, he might have turned it down earlier. The only excuse there can be for his injured innocence is that at least he had not received his pension from Mantua recently. After many letters asking for it, he dedicated his seventh book of madrigals to the duchess, obviously with an eye to gaining her influence in the matter. All he received in return was a necklace, a perfectly suitable token of her appreciation, no doubt, but not what he wanted. It is a wonder that he ever did anything for Mantua again, although this can scarcely excuse him for his dealings over *Andromeda*.

In all probability he kept on working for the Gonzagas, because in Mantua he could go on producing operas and intermezzos. At Venice there was no opportunity as yet to write dramatic music—or at least only occasionally, for in 1624 he had the chance to have his *Il combattimento di Tancredi e Clorinda* produced. This took place in the Palazzo Mocenigo, but we have no means of knowing whether the work was commissioned by Count Girolamo Mocenigo, or whether Monteverdi composed it first and looked round for a chance to perform it. One thing is certain: this time there were no embittering negotia-tions with a librettist. The poem was by Tasso, a scene from *Geru-salemme liberata*, and Monteverdi had known it for years. This in itself put it outside his normal development as an opera composer, for it was not meant as an opera libretto at all. The result is curious. The work is not really an opera or a ballet. It was performed by only three people, of whom one was a narrator and commentator. Instead of the festival orchestra of Mantua only a group of strings was used. The massive scenic designs were also not available. From this it is clear that Venice had little to offer even the most famous opera composer of the time.

His next commission, then, had to come from elsewhere—from Mantua again. Duke Ferdinand died in October 1626 and was succeeded by Vincenzo II, who was so ill that he spent most of his days in bed. Was it, as has been suggested, that Striggio as court chancellor was really in charge of affairs and could indulge his taste for Monteverdi's operas? Or was it that there was the usual desire for a festival when a new duke came to the throne? Whatever the reason, we find Monteverdi sending to Striggio a play (or a libretto) by Giulio Strozzi that he had been reading. It was called *Licori finta pazza inamorata d'Aminta* (Licoris who feigned madness, in love with Aminta), and it is significant that the idea of the opera came from Monteverdi himself. Moreover Strozzi, although a Florentine, was staying in Venice and was willing to adjust his play according to the composer's ideas. This time inspiration visited Monteverdi. He sent the original play to Mantua early in May 1627. By the end of the month he had permission to begin composition, but had to wait for the return of Strozzi from Florence to revise the libretto. Strozzi came back about 3rd June and work started. Monteverdi already had the part of Licoris planned to fit Margherita Basile, and was thinking of the other virtuosos. By the 20th the play was reorganized into five acts instead of the original three. By the end of July work was well advanced, and in spite of trouble with his eyesight and the sickness of the copyist, the score was dispatched to Mantua on 10th September, less than five months after its conception and not much more than three from the start of the composition. What happened after this is not known, and we have no record of a performance. The score is lost— a pity not only for the scholar but also for the musician. A work written at such a pitch of inspiration must have been a fine one.

The speed of composition would have been surprising in a young man, and Monteverdi was now sixty. Nor was *Licori finta pazza* the sum total of his work for the year. He set more of Tasso's *Gerusalemme liberata,* probably in some madrigalian form. And even before he had sent *Licori* to Mantua, he had received a commission from Parma to write music for an intermezzo to be performed during the celebrations of the marriage of Duke Odoardo Farnese to Margherita de' Medici. This time the libretto was sent to him from Parma. The subject was the strife between Venus and Diana, and Monteverdi saw the possibilities of the text at once. As usual, he found difficulties of detail, and since he was not conversant with the resources at Parma, nor was he a friend of his librettist, as he was at Mantua, he decided to go to Parma to discuss the problems at first hand. He already had an invitation from Striggio at Mantua, and having sought leave of absence from the procurators of St Mark's he left Venice immediately after the procession of the Doge and Senate to S. Giustina on 7th October. By the end of the month he was busy at work in Parma and was writing not only intermezzos but also music for a *torneo* or masque to be done during the wedding festivities. He was so busy that he wrote home asking for an extension of his leave. But the procurators were not pleased and wrote back on the 27th of November, demanding that he should 'come back to the duties of his post' at the earliest opportunity.[1]

No mean year's work, this, and possible only to a composer at the height of his powers. Monteverdi's cup of happiness must have been full when he received yet another invitation to return to Mantua as *maestro di cappella*. The composer's reply is especially revealing if we compare it with his angry refusal of seven years earlier. The anger now has gone. He even leaves his reply to the middle of his letter. No, he says, he is not going to move from Venice where he is secure and happy, where he has no burden of teaching and where his pay is regular and can be augmented with only a little extra work. If Duke Vincenzo really wishes to help him, perhaps he could use his influence to gain for him a canonry at Cremona so that he could return to 'his own earth' in his old age. It is a gentle letter and shows Monteverdi growing more graceful as he grows older. Such happiness was not to last. Even before Monteverdi was home in Venice to direct the Christmas music in St Mark's, disaster had happened. The composer tells us the story in a frantic letter to Striggio:

My son Massimiliano is in the prison of the Holy Office for having read three months ago a book which he did not know to be prohibited; but accused by the possessor of the book, who was already imprisoned and who had told him that the book contained only matter about medicine and astrology, he was immediately imprisoned by the Holy Father Inquisitor and wrote to me that if I gave a security of a hundred ducats as bail he would be released immediately.[2]

[1] Arch. Ven., *Proc. de Supra, Reg.* 194, fo. 40v. See Appendix E (page 203).

[2] Malipiero, op. cit., page 280.

With the aid of his Mantuan friend, Ercole Marigliani, Monteverdi found the bail and Massimiliano was soon out of prison. But the proceedings were by no means over. It was to be more than six months before the final examination proved the younger Monteverdi to be innocent—six months of fear and nervous waiting, with the threat of torture and imprisonment constantly overhead, six months of attempt-ted wire-pulling by the young man's father. In the meantime there was work to be done. Monteverdi went back to Parma in the New Year to finish off the intermezzos and the *torneo*. With the blessed fortune of a composer of festival music he was able to start rehearsing certain pieces and to try over anything that was doubtful months ahead of the actual performance. This finally took place in December 1628 at the ceremonial entry of Odoardo and his bride. Alas for the careful preparations—it rained. The firework display planned to take place in the main square was ruined, and Tasso's *Aminta* with Monte-verdi's intermezzos was performed there with a huge cloth acting as a roof.[1] Little wonder that observers have nothing to say about the music, although, as usual, the machines and the *balletto a cavallo* took the eye.

Any way Monteverdi was not there to hear how his music sounded under such conditions. Again he had tried to stay in Parma for Christmas. Again the procurators refused their permission. They were not going to have any inferior music since 'days of such solemnity cannot be celebrated without your presence', as they told Monteverdi.[2]

Back in Venice life changed but slowly. In 1627 Monteverdi's deputy at St Mark's, Alessandro Grandi, left to take charge of the music at Santa Maria Maggiore in Bergamo. In his place Giovanni Rovetta, a young man who had been first an instrumentalist and then a singer, was appointed. Less intimately concerning Monteverdi was the death of Duke Vincenzo at Mantua. His death was hardly unexpected, since he had been ill for some time. What was not so easily foreseen were the consequences. There was no male heir to the dukedom, and the son-in-law of old Duke Francesco Gonzaga

[1] A. Saviotti, 'Feste e spettacoli nei seicento', in *Giornale storico della letteratura italiana*, XLI (1903), pages 42 ff.

[2] Arch. Ven., *Proc. de Supra, Reg.* 194, fo. 50. See Appendix E (page 203).

assumed the title. Spain and Savoy both protested against the usurper, as they considered him. The Duke of Guastalla also pressed his claims to the throne. The 'usurper' relied on papal influence and Venice. France also took his part. In no time northern Italy was in an uproar. The bitter war which followed needs no description here. It culminated in the invasion of the imperial troops from north of the Alps and the sack of Mantua, with the cruel destruction of the Gonzaga treasures. After this Mantua was no longer a noble and important city. Its days of glory were over.

Monteverdi must have been doubly thankful that he had not returned there. In Venice, at least for the time being, things continued as before. Life seemed stable enough for the German composer Heinrich Schütz to come and learn the new art of opera and church music from Monteverdi. Monteverdi himself continued to practise his peaceful art. In 1628 he set to music some verses of Giulio Strozzi for a banquet given by the Venetian state to the visiting Grand Duke of Tuscany in the Arsenal. Two years later he collaborated again with Strozzi (who now seems to have become Striggio's successor as Monteverdi's librettist). This time the work was an opera, *Proserpina rapita*, produced on a grand scale in the palace of the Mocenigo family, with the usual machines and elaborate *décor*. In the same year Monteverdi collaborated with Manelli and produced an opera in Bologna.[1]

The political stability of Venice had protected her citizens from the effects of the war, and life was normal there as late as the summer of 1630. But the imperial troops had not only sacked Mantua; they had brought the plague into northern Italy. Venice took its usual stringent quarantine precautions and this delayed the arrival of the disease. The first cases appeared in the autumn and then it spread rapidly and fearfully. Soon no one would venture out of doors. The procurators of St Mark's even forwent the rents from their houses, for no one would

---

[1] Wolfgang Osthoff's recently published paper, 'Zur Bologneser Aufführung von Monteverdis *Ritorno di Ulisse* im Jahre 1640' (Vienna 1958), suggests that this is in fact not true, but that *Il Ritorno di Ulisse* was performed in Bologna ten years later. This information came too late for inclusion in this book.

collect them. The fathers of the church of SS. Giovanni e Paolo shut themselves up in their monastery. All their novices had died, and the organist Cavalli sought leave not to attend Mass on festival days for fear of the disease.[1] The school of San Rocco gave up its processions and no longer hired musicians to celebrate Masses for the souls of past wardens. Nor were the musicians of St Mark's spared. Several died, others were broken in health but survived. Monteverdi himself lived to see the end of the plague. So did his son Francesco (we have no news of Massimiliano). Both were almost certainly in St Mark's on 28th November 1631, when the Doge and Senate gave thanks for release from the scourge and 'there was sung a solemn Mass, composed by Sig. Claudio Monteverdi, *maestro di cappella*, the glory of our century, in which during the Gloria and Credo the singing was joined by loud trumpets (*trombe squarciate*) with exquisite and marvellous harmony'.[2]

After the strain of these times, it is not surprising that Monteverdi became ill, even though he had avoided the plague. He was well over sixty, and emotional strain affected him physically. A letter from the procurators tells us that in 1632 he went away from Venice for a time, perhaps to clear up affairs at Cremona after the destruction of the war. The address to which the letter was sent has been lost, but Monteverdi clearly had overstayed his leave:

To Sr D. Claudio Monteverdi, *maestro di cappella* to the Serene Signory of Venice.

MOST EXCELLENT AND REVEREND SIR,

We have received yours of the 7th instant, but no other letter, and we sympathize with you in your past illness, and the disturbing crimes which have happened in those parts; but it would please us to know that if you have recovered and brought to an end and put right your affairs, when would be the earliest at which you could return to the service of the church and to your post.[3]

[1] Arch. Ven., *SS. Giovanni e Paolo, Reg.* 12, fo. 206.

[2] E. Vogel, 'Claudio Monteverdi', in *Vierteljahrsschrift für Musikwissenschaft*, III (1887), page 89.

[3] Arch. Ven., *Proc. de Supra, Reg.* 194, fo. 81v. See App. E (page 203).

The plague and the war which had devastated the two cities where Monteverdi had made his home marked the end of an era, and at first sight it must have seemed like the end of the composer's activity. For the time being there was little enough opportunity for producing opera. Count Alessandro Striggio was still at Mantua, it is true, but the musical establishment there was sadly reduced. In the 1620's there had been no fewer than thirty musicians, including some famous singers. The roll of employees in 1637 shows that only eight singers were there—mediocrities of no lasting or wide fame.[1] In Venice things did not sink to this level. Monteverdi gradually brought the choir of St Mark's up to strength again, and the records show that the singers were on the whole paid rather better than before the plague. Even so the distinction of these musicians could not approach that of the previous decade. The flourishing school of church music composers had disappeared. And Monteverdi himself seems to have been more lax. Whereas at the beginning of his service in St Mark's he had been keen on daily services attended by the organists and all the singers, we find that several of them now took on outside engagements. One of the organists, Carlo Fillago, even took on the post of organist of SS. Giovanni e Paolo in addition to his own work in St Mark's, for which a few years earlier he had been reprimanded by the procurators.[2]

There are other signs of increasing age. Admittedly Monteverdi allowed his publishers to collect a volume of his works, the first for thirteen years; but this is a very slim volume of, for the most part, light fashionable airs, popular with both the Venetian presses and the public. On the title-page (as from the letter sent by the procurators in this year) we learn that Monteverdi has become a priest, a surprising step for a man of great independence—and one who, after the affair of Massimiliano, had every right to feel a little aloof from clericalism. The only two of his letters from these years which have come down to us show us that his thoughts on music were old-fashioned and had scarcely changed since his youth. The book promised by Giulio Cesare over twenty-five years earlier still occupied his mind:

[1] Arch. Gonzaga *Busta* 395.
[2] Arch. Ven., *SS. Giovanni e Paolo, Reg.* 12.

The title of the book will be: Melody, or the Second Musical Practice: by 'second' I mean considered in the modern manner, the First Practice being according to the old style. I divide the book into three parts corresponding to the three parts of Melody. In the first I discourse about the treatment of the words: in the second, about the harmony: in the third about rhythm. I think the book will be appreciated by the public because I discovered in practice when I was writing the *Lament of Ariadne,* not finding a book which explained to me the natural way of imitation, nor one which could show me that I should compose 'imitatively' except Plato, from which came so dim a light that I could hardly see it with my poor eyes, I discovered, I repeat, how great a fatigue one must undergo in doing what little I did of imitation, and therefore I hope that my work will not go unappreciated.[1]

We may be reasonably sure that he never completed this book. If he had, one wonders how many people would have been interested in this antiquated academicism.

Just as Monteverdi and Venetian music seemed to be peacefully declining, new life came into both. The immediate inspiration was the arrival of two composers and singers from Rome. Manelli and Benedetto Ferrari had been producing operas in Rome when political circumstances made it advisable to seek patrons elsewhere. With the illness and approaching death of Pope Urban VIII war looked very likely, and a stable society where opera could be treasured and supported seemed far more probable outside the Papal States—in Venice, in fact, where the two of them came with certain friends late in 1636. Monteverdi, who knew talent when he saw it, snapped them up for the choir of St Mark's,[2] although he must have known that their principal interests were not in church music.

In 1637 an opera house was opened with Manelli's *Andromeda.* The audience was mainly patrician, but since boxes were hired by various nobility and it was possible to buy tickets of admission for the pit, the S. Cassiano theatre can truthfully be said to be the first of the public opera houses. The idea caught on quickly and several others were

[1] Malipiero, op. cit., page 293.
[2] Arch. Ven., *Proc. de Supra, Chiesa Actorum* 144, 3rd October 1638.

VENETIAN SERENADERS

From a sixteenth-century engraving

opened in the succeeding years. Naturally Monteverdi was not to be left out of this feast of dramatic music. *Arianna* was revived in 1639 and he wrote a series of new works—*Adone*,[1] *Le nozze di Enea con Lavinia* and *Il ritorno d'Ulisse in patria*. As if to show that his energy was completely up to any demands upon it he wrote a *balletto* for the Duke of Parma; and published his eighth book of madrigals and a collection of church music. Neither of these books was a slender achievement. The contents of these thick volumes may have been composed earlier, but even the business of seeing them through the press must have been arduous and time-consuming. Finally, at the age of seventy-five, he composed an opera which we may well consider his masterpiece, *L'incoronazione di Poppea*.

What the public thought of these works of Monteverdi's astonishing old age we shall never know. Tangible appreciation of his genius can be found only in the proceedings of the procurators, who twice made him a present of a hundred ducats and finally gave him leave of absence to revisit his old home at Cremona. He spent about six months in 1643 travelling to the places where he had spent his earlier years, not only to Cremona, but to Mantua, where perhaps there were still friends. He returned to Venice only to die. He was taken ill on 20th November and on the 29th the registers of the Public Health tell us of his death: 'The most illustrious and Reverend D. Claudio Monte Verde, *maestro di cappella* of the church of S. Marco, aged 73 [*sic*], of malignant fever of 9 days duration: Doctor Rotta.' To quote the obituary written by Camberlotti: '. . . the news of such a loss upset and turned all the city to sadness and mourning, and was accompanied, not by singing from the choir of singers of St Mark's, but by their tears and weeping.' [2] He was buried in the church of the Frari, in the chapel of S. Ambrogio, after a requiem with music conducted by his pupil Giovanni Rovetta.

Even in an age which looked to the present rather than the past for its music Monteverdi's music and reputation were too great to die

[1] First attributed to Monteverdi in the early eighteenth century. The libretto does not mention the composer's name.

[2] Malipiero, op. cit., page 61.

immediately. His publisher, Vincenti, collected the manuscripts of his unpublished church music and any secular music which could be reconciled with modern taste, and published them in 1651. *L'incoronazione di Poppea* was performed in Naples in the same year. The procurators of St Mark's found that it was not so easy to replace such a distinguished man. They were careful to make inquiries all over Italy before making their appointment, and tried to persuade a distinguished middle-aged composer, Orazio Benevoli, to come from Rome, before being content to give the post to Rovetta.[1] But gradually memories faded, tastes changed. By the end of the century Monteverdi was forgotten. It is the pride of the modern historian that now we can justly write of his reward; for the reward of the composer of genius is immortality.

[1] Arch. Ven., *Proc. de Supra, Busta* 90, fo. 43.

CHAPTER IV

THE EARLIER MADRIGALS

THE heart of Monteverdi's music lies in his madrigals. There he tackled and solved what he conceived to be the problems of the composer. It is in his madrigal-books that we can observe his spiritual and technical development from his earliest youth to his old age. Just as Haydn's soul is laid bare in his string quartets, so is Monteverdi's in his madrigals; and this fact should make us cautious. No composer works in a medium for fifty years without taking it very seriously. The fact that the madrigal is by its nature a smaller-scale work than an opera or much of the church music does not mean we can dismiss it lightly.

The matter is further complicated by the very nature of the madrigal. The string quartet at least remains for a distinct grouping of players and has a certain unity of purpose from the beginning of its history to the end. The madrigal has not. Some madrigals were written, as we commonly imagine all of them were, for the intimate performance of amateurs, who played or sang their parts for the pleasure of *ensemble* performance. Others were destined for singing by virtuosos who were made to show off their voices to a highly critical audience. Others were meant as attempts at the revival of the glories of ancient Greece, aiming at the closest of unions between words and music, to be listened to by *literati* and sophisticated intellectuals. Nor have we exhausted the list. Some madrigals were essentially grandiose choral music, to be performed on a great festival day. Some were the choral episodes in plays and must be accounted dramatic music. Some were essentially light music, using dance rhythms and simple repetitive structures. All could be called madrigals; or, for the lighter music, canzonets. If, then, we are to understand Monteverdi's secular music we must do more than analyse it in an abstract way. It must be related to the audience or purpose for which it was designed.

Monteverdi's first audience at Cremona can hardly have been made up of the sophisticates and connoisseurs of the larger centres. It wanted pleasing and elegant music rather than anything profound or compli-cated; and this is precisely what we find in Monteverdi's earliest books of secular music. His first publication, which came out in 1584, was a slender book of canzonets for three voices—just the thing for a beginner, not only because its smaller forces made contrapuntal manipulation easier, but because the form was short and clear-cut. By this time the canzonet had lost its earlier connotation of parody and had become virtually a light-hearted, small-scale madrigal—with one difference. Morley tells us what it had become by the 1590's:

> The seconde degree of gravetie in this light musicke is given to Canzonets that is little shorte songs (wherin little arte can be shewed being made in straines, the beginning of which is some point lightlie touched, and everie straine repeated except the middle) which is in composition of the musick a counterfet of the *Madrigal*.[1]

The repetitive nature of the form is very important, for, combined with its small scale, it virtually confined the composer to a simple melodic growth with no complicated counterpoint and to a decidedly harmonic style. There is no room for word-painting or any complica-tion, nor for the tears and pathos of the serious madrigal.

Monteverdi's canzonets are, as we should expect, very like hundreds which were written in the last two decades of the century. Typically enough for a young man, he made his canzonets as complicated as he dared. Out of the score of numbers only two or three have the simple homophony which the more mature or less scrupulous masters of the time used. The close imitations which end *Io son fenice* are typical of his slightly academic attitude:

---

[1] *A Plaine and Easie Introduction to Practicall Musicke* (1597), page 180.

Conventional 'points' of the sort which filled the textbooks are also common, and Monteverdi does not hesitate to provide some teasing rhythms occasionally, either to express the words or for purely musical excitement. But although these things may indicate his provincial origins, the canzonets are charmingly traditional. Since they are short, the cadences occur frequently and give a clear diatonic harmony. The rhythms of the words suggest a music which constantly repeats short rhythmic patterns, and gives a pleasingly regular structure to each piece. Virtually no difficulties are given to either singer or player, and it can only have been the composer's lack of fame and the rivalry of scores of similar volumes which prevented the book from receiving a reprint.

The same charm appears in Monteverdi's first book of madrigals for five voices, which appeared three years after the canzonets. 'Madrigal' sounds more ambitious than 'canzonet', and from a technical point of view the manipulation of five voices involves a larger scale of writing and a greater challenge to the composer. Emotionally, however, there is no great advance in this book. The beginnings of the madrigals often remind us of the canzonets. *Se nel partir* has an opening phrase identical with *Chi vuol veder*; *Ch' io ami* is very like *Già mi credea*. The canzonet form seems to have remained in the composer's mind too. The traditional repetition of the last line of a madrigal is often interpreted by Monteverdi to mean a fairly strict repetition of a whole lengthy concluding section. Another reminder of the canzonets is the rhythms of the phrases. The gay, regularly accented fragments of melody are constantly used, and sometimes (as in *La vaga pastorella*), the whole madrigal seems to be centred on the rhythm of the music used for the opening words—another sign of small-scale, neat working.

Light-heartedness is the main mood of the madrigals, and the attitude to the poems reflects this. The verse either follows the pastoral convention, with the usual nymphs and shepherds, or it is lyrical, written in the first person with the sighs and tears of (as yet unrequited) love. None of it, except some poems of Tasso and Guarini, can claim any real distinction, and Monteverdi treats it for what it is worth: artificial and pleasing rather than profound. He has obviously learned all the tricks of conventional word-setting, such as the chromatic change to express *lasso*, triple time for *gioia*, the rest which represents a sigh before *deh* or *sospiro*. More than this, he has learned the art of contrast and has begun to explore the use of dissonance to express the pains of the lover. The strings of suspensions, without ever departing from traditional practice, nevertheless seem rather more prolonged and intense than is usual in madrigals of this time:

This passage from *Baci soavi* is magical in the way it excites us with its dominant sevenths, stiffens the tension with the major seventh, frustrates our feeling for tonality with an F♮, and makes it worse by turning this F into a dissonance before sinking helplessly into the cadence.

Such passages are quite common in this book, yet we still feel that the composer has not explored the possibilities of the poems fully. The reason is that the scale of the madrigal is hardly large enough to bear the strength of the passionate sections. He has not succeeded in using the variety of the five voices to develop his phrases to their full power. Too often a voice enters and disappears after a bar or two without doing anything more than repeat the opening of a motif; and Monte-verdi repeats rather than develops. In short, these madrigals are charming but little more, and it is not really surprising that the book had to wait for a reprint until 1607, when the composer's fame would ensure interest in his earlier music.

The second madrigal book also had to wait until 1607 for reprint-ing, but there is much less justification for this neglect. It came out in 1590, and it is remarkably mature and personal compared with the earlier works. It is not so much that the musical material is different. The canzonet rhythms and phrases permeate many of the madrigals also. The actual harmonies of the pieces contain nothing which cannot be found in his earlier music. Yet everything is slightly changed and more emotionally alive. What has happened is that Monteverdi has seen how to use the full *ensemble*, how to use the five voices to expand the phrases and sections. The beginning of *Non giacinti o narcisi*, for example, takes two short lines of the poem, opens with the first, overlaps it with the second and finally leaves the second in command. The cadence comes, and the third line takes up and expands the section with duet texture before yet another cadence. At this point Monteverdi would have rested content in his first book; in this one he is just beginning. He takes the melodic fragments already used and expands them. The first phrase, which had lasted only two bars at the beginning of the madrigal and was sung by two voices, is now given to the whole group of five. The phrase is spread over five bars and given a twist which takes it into a foreign key. The same thing happens to the second phrase and the third. A climax comes by bringing in the full group in a homophonic phrase, which is interrupted by two voices and then is itself repeated, slightly altered to make it more powerful. A little polyphonic working-out of new material follows, and then, canzonet-like, the opening phrase comes back and is developed in yet a new way, mingling with the middle section. Canzonet-like in principle this may be; but no canzonet on this scale was ever written, nor of this subtlety. The slight, anacreontic verse is given a new and more powerful meaning by the musician.

This madrigal is typical of the whole book, every number of which gives to its material and form the exact and inevitable working-out needed. To achieve this certainty of form Monteverdi has had to learn about two things. The first is the modern use of harmony. Instead of being little more than a by-product of counterpoint, it is now a very definite part of the musical structure. One symptom of this is the role of the bass part. In the earlier madrigals the bass had taken its place with the others, weaving the imitative fragments into the texture. This happens also in the second book; but there are long passages where the bass fills in harmonically and does nothing else. In *Non sono in queste rive* only twice does it take part in the imitation. The rest of the time it provides a foundation to the harmony in a way not very interesting for the singer but absolutely essential for the general effect.

The other development of skill is shown in the way the composer uses the variety of tone colour. Rarely do the voices enter one after another with their melodic points, except for special effects. Instead, Monteverdi brings them in to sing in pairs or threes, using the fifth voice to give a delicious unevenness and unexpectedness. The homophonic *tutti* nearly always comes as the first climax of a madrigal, and is used very sparingly thereafter. More usual are longish homophonic trio sections (such as we find at the beginning of *Dolcemente dormiva* or *Intorno a due vermiglie*).

Such technical developments are of the utmost importance, for they are precisely what makes possible a new certainty in matching the words. This time Monteverdi was more careful in choosing his poems. Eleven of the madrigals are settings of verses by Tasso, and this provided a great stimulus to the composer's imagination. Instead of the rather insipid and negative imagery of inferior lyrics, Tasso nearly always uses concrete images which can suggest music equally picturesque. How much better is the line 'Non si levava ancor' than 'Baci soavi, e cari'. It is no coincidence that the most famous madrigal of the book is a nature study where every line has an image in it. *Ecco mormorar l'onde*, indeed, is a gift to the composer. The murmuring of the waves, the rustling of the leaves, the height of mountains are things which naturally give an imaginative composer opportunities. If we quote some fragments of the tenor, we see how Monteverdi was inspired:

Equally vivid is the suggestion of a hunting scene in the opening of *S'andasse amor a caccia*, with its close canons and quasi-military rhythm. We may recall that the chase, with its opportunities for realism, had been a favourite Italian subject for musical setting as early as the fourteenth century:

The dawn setting of *Non si levava*, the calm of *Dolcemente dormiva* similarly inspire the composer to fluent and naturally imitative settings.

With this second book of madrigals Monteverdi spiritually left Cremona; and the difference between it and the first book makes us wonder whether the composer has not been studying more up-to-date models than his teacher Ingegneri could provide. The most probable explanation is that some of Giaches de Wert's madrigals had come into his hands, especially Wert's eighth book of madrigals for five voices which had appeared in 1586. There are too many similarities between these two sets of madrigals for a coincidence. Wert was a great friend of Tasso and set many of his poems. He also liked concrete images to make for easy tone painting, and in fact one of his madrigals, *Vezzosi augelli,* resembles *Ecco mormorar l'onde* very closely, even to the opening phrases setting the words 'mormora l'aura' and the melismas for 'cantan':

In another, *Qual musico gentil,* Wert sets *sospir* in exactly the way that we find in *E dicea*. The trio sections which Monteverdi finds useful are also clearly derived from Wert's works, as it was he who developed them in writing for the three ladies of Ferrara (see pages 9, 59). The very mood of Wert's madrigals is like those of Monteverdi's second book, never having the artificial gloom of the dissonant passages of the early works, but light, witty and very competent.

More than this, Wert about this time was developing something in which Monteverdi was to interest himself more and more. Wert was an academic composer in the sixteenth-century sense of the word, and was one of the favourite composers of the Accademia degli Intrepidi of Ferrara. We do not know much about the discussions of this body, as we do about those of the Florentine academies. What is certain is that it too was interested in interpreting the Greek theorists and that it had decided that the vital element in the creation of a modern music was a close relationship between words and music. Although in searching for audibility of the words it did not go so far as advocating monody, there can be no doubt from Wert's madrigals that some form of choral recitative was favoured. So in this eighth book we find constantly lines which repeat notes, less to give musical rhythms than to give exact declamations, and lengthy passages of homophony, not for musical effect, but to allow for the complete clarity of the words to the listener. The results are melodic lines which are quite the opposite of those required by polyphony. Not very interesting in themselves, they are explicable only in terms of the general effect as it appears to the listener.

In addition to these declamatory passages Wert was experimenting with other ways of verbal expression. Unlike many of the Ferrara composers, he had little interest in chromaticism and dissonance. Instead, he sought new effects by deliberately disobeying the tenets of smooth vocal writing and giving the singer huge awkward leaps which naturally conveyed great emotional tension. Sometimes he uses ninths and tenths in this way; at other places he merely arranges ordinary intervals into angular shapes which seem freakish and severe:

So · lo‿e pen · so · so‿i più de · ser · ti cam · pi

In these new paths Wert was one of the great pioneers, and the musical language of the later madrigal was much indebted to his work.

This extended discussion of Wert's style might seem superfluous if its influence on Monteverdi was as slight as it is in the second book of madrigals. The third book is so indebted to Wert that without some knowledge of his work it is impossible to see where Monteverdi was going. The young man's new book was published in 1592. Monteverdi had been about two years at Mantua, and suitably enough the book was dedicated to the duke as a thank-offering. Monteverdi now had a new and more musical audience, a group of composers of the most competent sort to put him on his mettle and more practised singers to perform his music. This perhaps explains the speed of production of this book. Normally Monteverdi was slow to gather enough works to publish; two years to complete twenty madrigals meant that he was working unusually quickly.

Only two of the madrigals seem to be Cremonese. *La giovinetta pianta* and *Sovra tenere herbette* are both in a light canzonetta style, with texts by unknown poets, treated with the gay rhythms and repeated sections we have noticed earlier. The rest are quite different in mood and treatment. The poets are Tasso or Guarini—both extremely fashionable at Mantua. The musical settings have obviously been influenced by Wert's declamatory technique. Almost all the madrigals in the book have some motifs which are based on a *parlando* monotone. Some begin with a solo voice declaiming the words:

Se per e - stre - mo_ar-do - re Mo - rir po - tes - se_un co - re

In *Vattene pur, crudel* we can see Wert's awkward leaps giving rise to a line which yet reminds us of Monteverdi's most mature writing:

Vat - te - ne pur cru - del con quel - la pa - ce che la - scia me

In fact, throughout the whole of this madrigal and its two succeeding parts Monteverdi is merciless to the singer, using leaps of the octave and of the sixth both ascending and descending, the upper registers of the voices and chromatic changes both in regular scale-wise passages and in sudden false relations. Add to this the onus on the singer to make the *parlando* phrases alive, and we see how far virtuoso singers have stimulated his imagination. In one madrigal particularly Monte-verdi is writing for the virtuosos. This is *O come è gran martire*, inspired (no less a word will do) by the three ladies of Ferrara. The form, with its trio opening and repeated *tutti* sections in the middle, is very like that of *Non giacinti o narcisi*. But Monteverdi's obvious enjoyment of three virtuoso ladies' voices is reflected in the declamatory phrases, the falling sixths, the top A's for the first soprano, the constant delight in crossing the parts to give the same chords new colours:

One thing we notice in this third book is the widening of the emotional range. Monteverdi still clearly likes the concrete image to give a nature picture. *O rossignol*, with its song of the nightingale, suggests delicate melismas; the waves which are the concluding image of *Vattene pur, crudel* give a charming swirl of sound. But to go with the declamatory lines and chromaticism the dissonant passages have returned. They are not more astringent than in the first book but they are much more effective. With the expansion of the scale these expressions of pain no longer seem exaggerated and out of place. In *Stracciami pur il core*, for example, there are two extended sections of slow-moving dissonance. The first one comes immediately after the beginning and is ushered in while the first, rather gay theme is still going on. The whole passage is held together by an ascending scale in the bass and the tautest chord involves merely a minor seventh. The atmosphere is relaxed in gentle counterpoint until the words 'Non puo morir d'amor' insist on passionate setting. Again we have the rising scale in the bass, and the passage is much shorter than the first one. But this is the climax of the madrigal, and minor seconds and double suspensions give an added burst before the composer finds the cadence and a happy ending.

In this madrigal and others Monteverdi shows how he can move from one emotion to another and mingle them together in a short space of time. This is something that all the great madrigalists of the later sixteenth century could do, Wert included. There is one great difference, however, between Wert and Monteverdi. Wert is more literary, Monteverdi more 'musical'. That is, Wert expects his words to make an appreciable part of the total impression, and music may at times be secondary. Musical forms are less important than the relentless pushing forward of the recitative. Monteverdi, on the contrary, makes the music express the words. He tries to find a musical equivalent, and words are important only in so far as they inspire him to musical forms and textures. A good example of this difference can be found in their two settings of *O primavera,* from Guarini's *Il pastor fido*. Wert takes a long section of Guarini's verse and sets it in a recitative-like manner with scarcely a repetition of the words. There is no attempt at finding the image of the poem and setting it in equivalent music. If you cannot hear the words you are lost. Monteverdi's setting, on the other hand, is practically a canzonet. He writes a huge eleven-bar opening on two lines of the verse, and then, in a magical way, gives sixteen bars of expansion and development, using all the possible permutations of motif, phrase and voice combination. One is lucky to hear the words at all—but this does not matter in the least. We know precisely what it is all about from a verbal fragment or two and the very expressive music. Of the two, Wert is the more advanced, Monteverdi the more attractive; and in spite of all Monteverdi's theorizing about the words being master of the music, even at this early stage it is possible to see that it is the composer's musicality which makes his art alive, not his capacity for putting words and music on an equal footing.

The third book today not only seems a great advance on his early music; it was also a success in its own day. It was reprinted in 1594 and 1600, no mean achievement for a book which clearly was not meant to be popular in the same way that Gastoldi's ballets were; and after Monteverdi had achieved real fame it went through five more editions. His publisher, Amadino, must have been waiting for another collection to send to the press. He had to wait eleven years before the fourth book of madrigals was ready. Why, one wonders, did the composer delay? Would it not have been better to keep his name before the public? Was he too busy to compose? The answer to the mystery seems to be that Monteverdi was peculiarly reluctant to publish his music at this time. When the fourth book did come out he mentions in the preface that he had hoped to dedicate some madrigals to Duke Alfonso d'Este II of Ferrara. Alfonso had died in 1597, so Monteverdi must have been composing before this. We know also from Artusi's criticisms that at least two of the madrigals in the book were composed as early as 1600. This suggests that he was composing continuously in these eleven years. Why, then, was he so loath to see his music in print?

The only explanation we can offer is that Monteverdi felt within himself a sense of progress and movement which made him unsure of his music. Certainly his fourth book is in an 'advanced' style which, although firmly rooted in his older manner, was likely to shock the conservatives. For these eleven years were amongst the most turbulent in the history of music. At Florence the monodists had finally been able to produce an opera, Peri's *Dafne,* and to follow it with the *Euridice* of Peri and Caccini. The latter composer's *Nuove Musiche* came out in 1602, and thereafter the monodic movement was securely launched. Monteverdi must have known all about these events; but we have no need to go even to Florence to find a change of mood and a new revolutionary fervour. In madrigal books published in these vital eleven years both Giaches de Wert and Benedetto Pallavicino showed how they too were concerned in the academic attempt to 'move the affections'. Wert's eleventh book is a remarkable achieve‐ment for a man of his years. In several numbers, and especially in *O primavera,* he takes a declamatory style as far as it will go. There are harsh dissonances, and in *Udite lagrimosi spirti* a know‐ledge of chromaticism which we would hardly have expected from him.

More interesting still is Pallavicino's sixth book of madrigals, which came out in 1600. Here a man who had been a reasonably conventional madrigalist a few years earlier suddenly explores chromaticism and dissonance. Many settings are of poems by Guarini also set by Monte‐verdi; and the older composer shows himself every bit as up to date as the younger. Without ever really doing anything which goes against established practice, Pallavicino manages to express the emotions of the poems with great force. The beginning of his setting of *Cruda Amarilli* is most powerful:

And he shows in the succeeding bars that he understands the way of building a climax which Monteverdi used in the earlier books, and by different combinations of voices gives breadth to the scale of the madrigal. His use of chromaticism is less satisfactory, for he is more rarely consistent in its use, and, we feel therefore, more experimental. But he is obviously trying to gain something of the quick emotional change of modern music. These are only two of the advanced traits of Pallavicino's madrigals. A further search reveals that the declamatory technique of Wert, the wide intervals of melody (he is even quite fond of the falling sixth we associate with Monteverdi), are also used to fulfil the demands of the verse. He is indeed a composer of the *seconda prattica*.

Did Pallavicino influence Monteverdi or was it the other way round? Or perhaps Wert was the real teacher of them both. We do not know. What we do gain from our knowledge of the work of these Mantuans is a sense of a musical world in turmoil. We need not even think of the work of Gesualdo in Ferrara (he had married the Este princess in 1594 and must have started his experiments at this time), or Marenzio, to realize that there was a great deal to make Monteverdi unsure of the value of his music, to make him wonder if he was working on the right lines, and so to make him delay the publication of his madrigals. If he had such fears, there was little need of them. His fourth book is perhaps the most superb and consistent of all of them: it is the work of a complete master. Although the book's greatest achievement may seem to be the added power which dis, sonance and chromaticism give to the deeply felt sad numbers, there are a number of bright, happy pieces which are superb. Even a sense of quiet bitter-sweet irony can be heard in *Ohimè*. There is a complete, ness of emotional power which touches life at many points, and in each madrigal Monteverdi has a control of the words which means that he can follow their images and feelings in an incredibly exact way.

To show this at work we may take *A un giro*. At first sight it looks like a frothy piece in the manner of the Tasso settings of Book II. The word 'giro' (turn) produces a picturesque motif, and we begin with a little duet for sopranos with the bass filling in the harmony. The next line of verse is built round the word 'ride' (smile) and is worked out accordingly. The next section is an image of the sea and winds lightly moved (most reminiscent of *Ecco mormorar l'onde*), and Monteverdi again paints delicately. The mood changes: 'Only I am left to pine.' A sudden change of motion and the harmony is again conventional. Then Monteverdi pushes the shaft home, as the poet does: 'My death is born from your cruelty.' The dissonance here is as harsh as it is unexpected. A declamatory line with two voices on the same note suddenly becomes a slow line of continuous suspensions:

This movement from unison to dissonance merely by moving the line up a tone or semitone is a favourite device in this book, and always surprises because of its sudden change from the most perfect of con, sonances to one of the keenest discords. Nevertheless, both in this madrigal and in others, after its use as a weapon of surprise the scale of the piece gradually allows the section to expand, and with its repetition the dissonant phrase loses its sharpness and evaporates into another motif and the peace of the word 'death'.

Technical perfection, and especially perfection of form, gives Monteverdi a command of this kind; but it is an insight into musical imagery, a knowledge of where to place the emphasis and how to find an equivalent of the inner meanings of words, which gives this fourth book of madrigals a delight hard to find in any madrigal book by any other composer. *Sì ch'io vorrei morire* is an indecent little piece of verse, in which the love kiss (veiled as usual in the image of 'death') and the way to its climax—now sweet and almost restful, now passionate and energetic—are hinted at, until a state of rest comes at last. It is not a distinguished poem by any standards—little more than a play on words which scarcely arouses our feelings at all. It is indeed a standard of Monteverdi's mastery that he has managed to give added meaning to a poem without any concrete images to inspire him. The neutral opening does not attempt to paint 'morire'—quite deliberately because it is a point of rest. A *tutti*, by a chromatic twist, increases the tension; and then there is a huge section on the 'cara e dolce lingua' in which the lingering weakness and tenseness of love are given memorable expression by the continuous dissonance (usually with three adjacent notes of the scale sounded together), after which comes a falling section of more conventional suspensions as the lover feels himself 'dying'. He has a sudden return to life with a short rhythmic motif, and a feeling of haste is conveyed by a canon at the half-beat and a string of suspensions, repeated in one form or another three times, with a third voice finally exclaiming ecstatically 'Ahi bocca! Ahi baci! Ahi lingua!' until the great climax; and, with a touch of mastery, the peace of the aftermath is given perfect expression by a repetition of the opening.

Sì ch'io vorrei has an emotional life which could in 1603 be found only in the most intense modern madrigals; yet there is nothing in it which is revolutionary. Even the passage with the three adjacent notes of the scale held together simultaneously can actually be justified by conventional rules. This cannot be said of *Ohimè*. The very opening of the madrigal contains harmonies which are impossible by ordinary standards:

The effect is splendid. Again the subject is the spurned lover; and this
time dare we take his sighs too seriously? The dissonance is not
extended enough and therefore does not sound too severe. There is
merely a tang of desire in these strange unaccented chords. This is
carried through the madrigal in a magical way. When we arrive at
the climax, 'Alas, why do you wish him who sighs to die?' the
dissonances, far from being the astringencies of *Si ch'io vorrei*, are
accumulations of passing notes which do not always arrive at their
destination and which therefore attract attention to themselves; and
they are never prolonged, never harsh. Nor is the ending full of the
passion which Monteverdi has at his command. Instead the 'thousands
and thousands of sighs' are given life by a series of false relations which
convey a sense of indeterminate tonality. A pedal note in the final bars
gives some light dissonance, and the concluding 'ohimè's' gently
remind us of the opening. The mood of the music is again the exact
mirror of the words. The bantering, never too passionate love of both
is a typical offshoot of the pastoral conventions. It is often difficult to
believe in the grand amours of Thyrsis and Cloris. Monteverdi has
gone one better: he has written the music of flirtation without becoming purely artificial (for his motifs are anything but conventional),
while at the same time remaining always full of feeling.

If I have discussed the emotional life of these madrigals in detail,
reading into them perhaps—as is always the danger—things which are
not really there, the reason is that the technical resources of this and the
fifth book of madrigals are so interesting for the development of music
that Monteverdi's masterful psychology is sometimes forgotten. But I

cannot leave this book without commenting on its musical resource too, for the volume is a key to Monteverdi's subsequent development. One thing we notice is that the 'academic' traits come to their full expressiveness in these madrigals. Chromaticism, for example, is nowhere better integrated into the madrigal than in the last number of the book, *Piagne e sospira*. The rising chromatic scale of the opening acts almost as a *canto fermo*, around which the different emotions and different musical motifs are wrapped. At the end, when the final chromatic fragment is no longer used, a chromatic change in a chordal passage is as expressive as any harmonic use of chromaticism could be. There is none of the enigmatic suddenness of Gesualdo's chromatics. Everything is musically developed to its fullest extent.

Similarly, Wert's experiments in *parlando* declamation are used perfectly here and no longer seem at all experimental. A great deal of *Voi pur da me* is written in homophonic, quickly moving declamation in which the words are perfectly audible. What Monteverdi has done is to make every harmonic change significant, every change of texture contribute to the ebb and flow of tension. More than that, the expressiveness of melody now can be heard at its clearest, for the top lines (usually two of them) use the slides and ornaments, the capacity to hold notes, to make expressive pauses, all of which Monteverdi had learned from the virtuoso singers of Mantua. In *Sfogava con le stelle* he uses the declamatory style in yet another way. Here is the extreme of verbal clarity in the *ensemble* madrigal; in six places he does nothing but indicate the chords to be sung, leaving the rhythms to the singers, who must chant them as they would the psalms written in *falso bordone*. Nothing could be simpler; but this is used not just to give clarity to the words, but to make the succeeding passages in counterpoint more overwhelming. As one acute observer has found, the neutral words, the words which have no direct expressive power, are left in chant. Those which are personal, evocative and emotional are given the full power of expressive music—all the modern harmonies, the nervousness of ornaments and strange leaps in melody.

These two madrigals are typical of the whole book in this way. The power of harmony—not necessarily dissonance, but of chromatic changes and modulation—and virtuoso melody have now in fact done away with real counterpoint. There are many passages which could be performed by a solo voice with a keyboard accompaniment—even more by two voices and keyboard. Something would be lost, because the colouring of the voices and the changes of texture are important. Yet the essentials would be there. There is no doubt that Monteverdi is now writing music for the aristocratic listener rather than the aristocratic performer. No groups of dilettantes could possibly perform it adequately. The older ideal of the madrigal is as dead as it is in the madrigals of Gesualdo or the monodies of the *camerata* composers.

The fourth book of madrigals was successful and had to be reprinted in 1605 and 1607, to go no further (it is interesting to note that a great deal of 'modern music' was seemingly popular, for Pallavicino's sixth book also went through several editions quickly). Perhaps it was this that encouraged Monteverdi to bring out another book soon after. The fifth book appeared in 1605. At least one of its numbers had been composed five years earlier and another had been known to Artusi in a manuscript copy for some time. So it seems that part of the contents of the fifth book was composed about the same time as those of a previous collection. There are two changes to note, the first of which might appear a purely technical one. A *basso continuo* part is supplied. For over half the contents it is not necessary; for the remaining ones it is essential, and these are therefore rather different in technique. We must not exaggerate the immediate effects in sound. Probably madrigals of earlier volumes were performed with instrumental accompaniment and with soloistic decorations such as we find in these new madrigals. Nevertheless the conscious use of a keyboard accompaniment leads to very new conceptions, and these madrigals are original enough to open a new chapter in the history of the form. The other novelty for a Monteverdi madrigal book was the complete elimination of the canzonet style. Even the highly serious fourth book had its lighter numbers, for instance, *Io mi son giovinetta*. The 'conventional' madrigals (as we may call those which do not use the *basso continuo* as an essential ingredient) of Book V are all sad. Some of them seem almost emotionally overwrought. The laments of the various lovers in Guarini's *Il pastor fido* are the main choice of verse, and they are treated as vehicles for great musical intensity, without any suggestion of that teasing not-too-serious pastoralism of which Monteverdi is sometimes capable.

The immediate result of this emotionalism is that the harmony of some of the madrigals is more dissonant, and stranger in the way it uses false relations; and it was these things that Artusi attacked in his various books and pamphlets. It was to be expected that he would direct an attack on *Cruda Amarilli*, for there is one bar which is very unconventional:

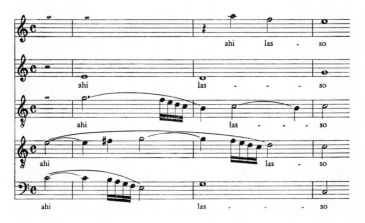

Even so, Artusi's attack is more on a paper reading than on the actual sound. If we compare Monteverdi's opening, it is much less dissonant than Pallavicino's. It is unusual for its ornaments, fully written out; but Artusi must have heard things like that many times from singers adding improvisatory *gorgie*. There are other pin-pricks of harmony, but again they are more 'difficult' on paper than in sound. For the most part, the madrigal is more conventional than many in the fourth book, both in its melodic motifs and in its treatment of them.

More worthy of Artusi's attack, for it is one of the greatest of Monteverdi's madrigals, was *Era l'anima mia*. Guarini's first image is of the soul at its last hour. Its double meaning is so ordinary in the verse of the period that we hardly think about it. Monteverdi seems to take it at its face value, and using the lower voices (and the lowest registers of them) gives a picture of frightening intensity. Long-held pedal notes, over which two voices in thirds give the effect of modern dominant preparation, and frequent false relations never allow the tension to drop. If we wish to feel how intense this is, it is only necessary to compare the passage with a setting by Pallavicino:

The soul is reprieved by a glimpse from a more blessed spirit and Monteverdi brings in his upper voices with almost angelic effect. Thereafter the verse proceeds by a series of double meanings, by sighs and threatened deaths. The music breathes life into the conventions, and by long pedals and dissonant passing notes comes to a memorable climax. These two madrigals could well have come from the fourth book; in psychological power and emotional grandeur they seem to complete a phase in Monteverdi's work.

The other 'conventional' madrigals, with one exception, seem less interesting and, for Monteverdi, more experimental. There are two long cycles of linked madrigals to verse from *Il pastor fido*, both of which seem to have gone back to the ideals of Wert. Both are obviously concerned less with madrigalian expressiveness than with the audibility of the words. Almost the whole of the first part of *Ecco, Silvio* is written in homophonic declamation. There are varied groupings of voices and some striking harmonic changes; but the sacrifice of expressiveness has been great. In the subsequent sections the texture is adhered to less severely, but nowhere in the works is there anything of the sheer magic we find in some of the earlier madrigals. What we do notice is a great interest in the development of the melodic line—by now the upper melody throughout. The lower parts often consist of filling in of little independent interest. Monteverdi is developing a definite attitude to this, and a number of personal mannerisms have appeared. One is the use of a descending leap of a sixth which comes at moments of crisis. It is possible to find this in earlier works (even in Book III), but it now happens so often as to become almost a cliché. Another is a suspension which resolves irregularly and draws attention to itself by leaping to an unexpected note of the new chord. Another is the use of sequence to press home a phrase; and another an occasional expressive ornament. The beginning of *Dorinda, ah dirò* is a good example. First a short phrase; then a repetition of it higher up; then an ornamental repetition and an obsessional development of the three notes of the scale before the section is complete—these are the stages of melody building:

Do-rin - da, Do-rin - da_ah di - rò mi - a, ah di - rò

mia Se mia non se - i

This is more skilful and more deeply felt than anything we find in Wert's recitative madrigals; yet it is little compensation for the splendours of Monteverdi's natural madrigal style. There is, how, ever, one exception. This is *O Mirtillo*. It is certainly written in the recitative madrigal style, and with little trouble it could be reduced to a monody, for the important melody is always in the top part and there is always a clear bass part, even in the trio sections. The melody is of the most expressive kind of declamation. The downward sixth leap begins the madrigal and sets the atmosphere at once. The suspension which resolves irregularly comes several times. But more than this, Monteverdi uses the complete resources of the madrigal. The chains of suspensions which we have seen in earlier books now dominate the first climax. Words and phrases are repeated to give scale to the madrigal, which never seems restricted or in the least experimental. As several observers have pointed out, it is the first of the great laments and the true model for the *Lamento d'Arianna*, which was in turn to set a fashion for many years and many composers. Although rather simpler in psychology than some of the madrigals of the fourth book, it is a good example of what can be done with the new manner.

The continuo madrigals seem to demand a new chapter. Typically enough they start in the middle of a madrigal book, for Monteverdi's music progresses so naturally that any division is artificial. The division of his madrigals into two is merely for our convenience, since the introduction of the *basso continuo* is a suitable place for us to recapitulate the excitement of the 'new music' which had been so proudly proclaimed by the Florentines a few years earlier, and which used this new device as an integral part of its nature. Yet if the glories of Greece had been re-created by anyone it was by Monteverdi, using the older techniques or extensions of them. His claim to be a descendant of Rore and the rest was quite justified, and already he could claim to be by no means the least of the moderns.

As a writer of conventional madrigals Monteverdi stays somewhere between Marenzio and Gesualdo. He is a less polished composer than the former, whose music is often the accurate mirror of the anacreontic verse he sets. Monteverdi is too rugged, too interested in human beings to be able to believe in the pastoral convention. Yet he is too much a musician to be a purely psychological composer like Gesualdo, who seems to have no interest in musical device. In one way he excels both of them. In his range of emotion he is greater than either. He can be passionate and pessimistic, gently ironic or supremely gay in turn. We have no right to be surprised when he turns out to be a great opera composer. His madrigals, with their range of human interest and their variety, from introversion to almost pure objectivity, have prepared the way thoroughly; and if at times we seem to undervalue these works, the only reason can be that we do not devote to their performance the virtuosity which their composer expected. There is no other barrier to our understanding.

CHAPTER V

MADRIGALS WITH BASSO CONTINUO

THE *basso continuo* was one of those inventions which had an influence on the history of music far beyond any expectations of its originators. It came out of the specific needs of certain composers. Some of them were mundane. Viadana, *maestro di cappella* at Mantua Cathedral, had the need for a notation which would allow the organist to fill in gaps in the harmony when the singers were few. Motets written deliberately for one or two or three solo voices required a well-organized accompaniment if the music was not to sound thin and weak. A notation which allowed for the cheap production of keyboard parts was a godsend to him and many another musician working in difficult conditions.

There were also more noble reasons, especially those of the Florentine academics, who, in their attempt at reviving the glories of Greek music, came to the conclusion that the decadence of modern music was really caused by polyphony, since it 'lacerated the poetry' (as one of them put it), and that the only way of uniting words and music on equal terms was for a single voice to be used. The words would then be clear and the singer could 'move the spirit', or appeal to both the intellect (through the words) and the emotions (through the music). Unwilling to sacrifice the power of harmony altogether, they too sought a notation which would make quite clear the subordinate role of the accompaniment. Their attempt was a revival of Greek music; their success, a new kind of music for the court. It is no coincidence that some of the first composers of the new music were singers. The very nature of monody was to glorify the virtuoso, and since for some

74

time the tastes of Ferrara, Mantua and the other courts had been for the nimble throats of Laura Perperara, Adriana Basile and the rest, it is no wonder that the new music became fashionable. The first song-books came out in 1602, and within ten years monody was in constant demand.

The earliest books contained two types of song. One, the most important in the first fifteen years or so, preserved the name 'madrigal'; and with good reason, for it followed the main principle of the later polyphonic madrigal—that the words were to be expressed in the greatest possible detail. The new methods were admittedly a little different, although they too had their origins in the older style. In some madrigals the conception was to provide an exact declamation for most of the song, repeating the words little, if at all, and saving expressive music for important words or phrases. This expressive-ness took the form of virtuoso ornamentation, which now became surpassingly involved and demanding. In other madrigals exact declamation was sacrificed a little for a continuous *arioso* movement with climaxes brought about by jagged intervals and dissonant harmonies. Some of these *arioso* madrigals are really very like the more advanced madrigals in Monteverdi's fourth and fifth books, in that these would have sounded very similar if performed with a single voice and instrumental participation. But the newer style, as it was first conceived, had several disadvantages. Whereas the lightly con-trapuntal texture of Monteverdi enforces both a fairly strict rhythm and a sense of formal development, these *continuo* madrigals had a tendency to be a little amorphous and uninteresting, especially if sung with the free *rubato* which some of the composers advocated. Admit-tedly this followed up the ideas of the theorists in so far as it threw emphasis on the words; but as time went on the music conquered, and the repeating of verbal phrases, the use of refrains and other devices began to give a new attractiveness.

The *continuo* madrigal was inconceivable without the taste for splendid virtuoso singing. The second type of monody was designed for broader popularity. The aria, as it was called, had nothing to do with the ancient Greeks. It was the natural descendant of the ballett and the canzonet, both of which were sold by the score (Monteverdi's among them) in the latter decades of the sixteenth century. The simplest arias are sharp in rhythm, clear-cut in harmony and tonality, and—so that they should be unforgettable—strophic in their treatment of the words. They set verse which one writer has aptly characterized as 'amorous baby talk' to the lightest of tuneful music. Some arias were, it is true, a little more complicated. These were written in the form which we know as the strophic variation. Each verse of the poem was set to slightly changed music, but the bass is kept the same throughout—a tether by which the melody maintains its general shape. The composer may manage to get in more detail of tone painting, but the general mood is still gay and it is no surprise that these two types of aria eventually defeated the more serious madrigal and drove it from the song-books.

What had Monteverdi to do with such new ideas? Not much, is the answer: or rather, not much while the ideas were really new. Certainly he was interested in the Greek philosophers and in the possibilities of monody. But the glories of the ancients were not necessarily to be found in this music of singers and dilettantes. Like most professional composers, he was slow to take to the solo madrigal and aria. When he did use the *continuo*, it is typical that it should interest him more as a new technical means, rather in the practical way of Viadana than in the experimental way of the Florentines; typical also that when he finally took the plunge, in the last six madrigals of Book V, the general effect is perhaps more conservative than some of the daring numbers of his Book IV. The first of the *continuo* madrigals, *Ahi, come a un vago sol*, is a masterpiece. The poem belongs to the usual kind of love verse, with all the conventionally affective words—sighs, wounds and so on. Monteverdi writes music which gives them vivid expression. In a *continuo* madrigal, melody is especially important, and the opening duet for tenors uses all the resources of florid ornamentation in much the same way that Caccini's madrigals of his *Nuove Musiche* use them. With a second voice to enrich both harmony and sonority, the effect is superb and much more powerful than anything Caccini ever wrote:

The phrasing, too, is magical—now long and sustained, then suddenly quickened emotionally with short, more broken fragments of
melody. The bass moves comparatively slowly as the interest lies
completely in the tenor parts, but because of the continuous movement
in these there is never any feeling that the rhythm has collapsed, as
there sometimes is in early operatic monody. This tenor duet is in four
sections, the first very long and culminating in a splendid decorative
climax, the second still decorated but somewhat shorter, the last two
becoming progressively more direct in melody and more concentrated.
To separate them is a *tutti*—a refrain which happens four times in all,
slightly altered each time in texture but otherwise the same, with the
final *tutti* extended by a coda using harmonies over a pedal note,
reminiscent of earlier madrigals. Indeed, the refrain is altogether like
part of one of the madrigals from the fourth book, contrasting with the
tenor duet by its rhythmic directness and mobile bass. Nor is any part
of the madrigal very different from the earlier madrigals which use the

trio texture freely. There are just two significant changes. One is the rondo form—a form which is clearly melodic, and much more obvious than the earlier developments from the canzonet. The other is the sectionalism which results from giving all the trio sections to one group of voices and from decisive cadences at each change of texture. This interest in forms, which derives from Monteverdi's earliest days, stands him in good stead. We have only to look at the motets of his Mantuan colleague Viadana, who was trying to solve the same problems at the same time, to see how well Monteverdi has avoided the amorphousness which was the trouble in much early *concertato* music.

In *T'amo, mia vita* we find the same inventiveness in the face of this problem. The verse is simple enough. The beloved says 'I love you', and the lover is happy. Here Monteverdi gives the words of the beloved to a soprano, who sings them several times, while each time the lover, represented by the three lower voices, gives a different cry of joy and tenderness. The sections are short and the bass is more consistently in motion, so that everything sounds quite conventional. Yet the way the upper voice is used leaves no room for doubt that a soloist is needed, a soprano who can hold a note and make it expressive. The lower voices are full of chromatic changes, effective if perhaps less subtle than those used in Book IV; and the declamatory chattering in quavers, although at first sight not interesting in itself or very exactly matching the rhythm of the words, is psychologically right. The amplification of the opening motifs into a concluding *tutti* rounds off the piece perfectly.

After these successes (the fifth book went through seven editions in ten years) we might expect another madrigal book to follow; but between the opera and his emotional troubles Monteverdi can have had little time, and indeed the only volume of any sort was a collection of trios made by his brother, Giulio Cesare. These are called *Scherzi musicali* and came out in 1607. Scholars have devoted a great deal of attention to the volume, mainly in trying to find out what Giulio meant by referring in the preface to the *canto alla francese*—a term which turns up again in some of Monteverdi's motets. To relate these slight trios to *musique mesurée* and French academic ideas is to take these songs too seriously. They belong to an Italian tradition—a Mantuan tradition even. They are the natural successors of Gastoldi's *balletti*, which were popular as early as the 1580's. In particular, Gastoldi's *Balletti a tre voci*, which came out in 1594, are very near in atmosphere, texture and phrasing to Monteverdi's *Scherzi musicali*; and since they were designed for playing and singing together, they may well have sounded like the later works. Typically, Monteverdi is rather more complicated. He likes the *hemiolia* rhythms, which indeed intrigued some of the writers of the monodic ariettas and were to become increasingly fashionable:

Da - mi - gel - la Tut - ta bel - la, Ver - sa, ver - sa quel bel vi - no. Fa che

ca - da La ru - gia - da Di - stil - la - ta di ru - bi - no.

Monteverdi also provides a short instrumental *ritornello* between the verses of each song, in most pieces seeming to develop the themes of the song lightly. Some of the songs are very charming, especially *Lidia spina* with its appealing little ending alternating between major and minor. Others are too regular and too short-breathed to satisfy. In this sort of light music many composers were as good as Monteverdi, and we must look elsewhere for his true development.

The sixth book of madrigals appeared in 1614 when Monteverdi was firmly installed in Venice, but its contents are the work of his Mantuan years. A madrigal book for five voices looked old-fashioned in 1614, even if there was a *basso continuo* part; and it is not surprising that there was not the tremendous success for it that there had been for the fifth book. Even so, it is a splendid volume. The two main works are a madrigalesque arrangement of the *Lamento d'Arianna* and the lament of a shepherd on the death of his nymph. There are also two Petrarch settings, both in a reasonably conventional, almost *a cappella* style, and a number of *concertato* madrigals after the manner of the last six in Book V.

The laments are both examples of Monteverdi's finest music. The *Arianna* arrangement was criticized by Doni on the grounds that it spoiled a work which was essentially expressive solo music. Be that as it may (and we must remember that we have neither seen the opera nor possess the complete score of the *scena*), it is easier for us to understand the popularity of the piece from the madrigal version than from the monody. The scale of the madrigal is nearer our expectations; the monody, as printed by Gardano, with its chorus interpolations cut out, seems too small. Again, the harmony which the composer uses in the madrigal is more powerful than any we can conjure up from the *basso continuo* part of the monody, if only because the sustaining power of the voices is so much greater than on any accompanying instrument; and this is important, for the madrigals are clearly very much in the tradition of Book V. Moreover, the arrangement is a great deal more than a thickening out of the monody. In the very first section, for example, the refrain, 'Lasciatemi morire', with its acid dissonance, comes twice in the monody to make up a neat *da capo* form which is entirely satisfactory. In the madrigal version, it bursts in yet another time. After the opening (slightly lengthened to allow all five voices to enter and expand the phrases) the second section, 'E chi volete voi' acts as an episode for three voices with a dissonant climax of its own. Then the first phrase of 'Lasciatemi morire' returns, but is never allowed to complete itself, as 'E chi volete voi' comes in with renewed tone on the full *ensemble*. Only then is a *da capo* allowed to bring a state of despair and rest. In a way this is more expressive than the original, and although the very rhythms of the later parts of the lament hardly seem appropriate for domestic musicmaking, it is one of the heights of Monteverdi's madrigal writing.

Monteverdi's arrangement of the piece is so good that there is only one thing which might make us suspect that the lament is part of a longer work. It is too intense. From its dissonant beginning to the turbulent final section there is scarcely a relaxed moment, and this robs the piece of some of the pathos which may well have been part of the original *scena*. In arranging the lament Monteverdi has clearly kept the moments of highest tension and cut away the rest. From this point of view, the other lament, *Incenerite spoglie*, is formally better, for it works towards its climaxes from points of rest and alternates the tragic exclamations with less subjective phrases. Several observers have pointed out that it would be possible to arrange the piece as a monody without much alteration, and this is certainly true of the first section, in which the tenor stands out against the *tutti* and in declamatory phrases sings of the shepherd's grief.

But this, after all, is something which would be said of many of the declamatory madrigals of Wert and a number of the madrigals from Monteverdi's earlier books, and it is as the successor of these that we must discuss *Incenerite spoglie*. It opens rather like *Era l'anima mia* with a chant setting the scene—the shepherd weeping beside the tomb of his beloved. His cry 'Ahi lasso' breaks in on the chant with a madrigalian symbol which is all the more effective for its context:

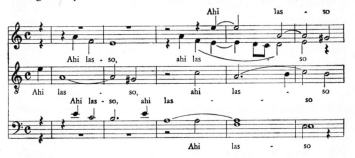

Then in a manner very similar to the madrigals in Book IV the declamation returns, but with varied vocal colouring in different trio combinations. In one way these trios are very different from the earlier madrigals. There is no attempt to make the words clear, and often the bass part of the trio sings a completely different phrase from the others.

The mastery of Book IV, however, is in evidence. Using but a single line of the poem, Monteverdi builds up a tense atmosphere, now allowing the phrase to complete itself, now breaking it off, now giving it a new ending or speeding it up to bring it to the cadence. In the later sections Monteverdi adds a device most affecting in its simplicity. While most of the voices declaim continuously, one or two voices break off to exclaim 'Ahi morte' or 'Ahi Corinna', so insistently that the other voices too in the end take up the plaint. Also unlike the earlier madrigals is the comparative lack of dissonance. Nor is chromaticism used a great deal, either for sudden changes or large-scale modulations. Only towards the end of the fourth section is there anything like the harmonic astringency which is often associated with Monteverdi, and here again the very restraint in the rest of the cycle makes the moment of anguish even more agonized, as the double suspensions and pedal notes bring the musical climax. The result is very different from the *Lamento d'Arianna*. Less obviously powerful, the cycle is by no means inferior, and it is as moving in its pathetic helplessness as any of Monteverdi's madrigals.

These two laments, with two shorter numbers in much the same mood, take up about two-thirds of the book. It is tempting to see reflected in them the emotions of Monteverdi's later troubled years at Mantua. But just as Beethoven could write an *Eroica* and a fourth symphony together, so we find in this sixth book of madrigals a lighter vein which shows that Monteverdi was still the complete master of all expressive music. In one of the conventional madrigals he even returns to the development of the canzonet. *Zefiro torna* goes back to Petrarch for its poem, and an *a cappella* texture for its music. Conventional, however, is not quite the word for it, because its first section is in triple time, something very rare in *a cappella* madrigals, and the decorations in the upper voices which round off each section never happened in former times. Both are reflections of the newer monodies—the triple time now a favourite for ariettas, the ornaments conventional for all music. All the old skill is there, with the contrasts of the poem brought out between lengthy sections as always, and the ending 'Sono un deserto e fere aspr'e selvagge', is a recollection of Wert's setting of another Petrarch sonnet, *Solo e pensoso*.

There are no such backward glances in the style of *Qui rise Tirsi*, a joyous *concertato* madrigal and a proper successor to *Ahi, come a un vago sol*. The form again is a series of duets and trios separated by the *tutti* singing an ecstatic refrain, 'O happy memory and happy day'.

This little refrain is in the style of the *tutti* sections of the madrigals of the earlier books (it is very like *O Mirtillo*). The duet sections, on the other hand, are modern and show an increasing grasp of the new medium. Instead of the mainly declamatory style of *Ahi, come a un vago sol*, Monteverdi enjoys the resources of florid melody to the full, using dotted rhythms and roulades with the greatest freedom. These ornaments appear consistently throughout the phrases, forming sequences which give a firm shape to the melody. The duet texture itself is used splendidly. Plain writing in thirds and sixths which fills out the harmony is the staple fare; but instead of the rather dull results which come through the excessive use of these cloying intervals in the *Scherzi musicali*, Monteverdi now knows exactly how to offset them by breaking forth into counterpoint. How effective, for example, is the following climax to a duet section for tenors after about eight bars of movement in thirds; it comes about not just because of the florid melody but also because the second tenor has simply moved one beat later than the first:

In spite of this more cheerful music the total impression of the volume is one of tragic power, which seems to be Monteverdi's more familiar vein. To this period we must also ascribe yet another lament, a monody called *Lamento d'Olimpia*.[1] Written in three sections to words inspired by a scene in Ariosto's *Orlando furioso*, it is clearly an offshoot of the success made by the *Lamento d'Arianna*. The same short, memorable phrases, the same use of emotional falling intervals, the same tendency for the harmony and melody to be slightly at odds make it a fine piece. It is a worthy companion to the similar laments of contemporary composers such as d'India.

Yet pure monody of this sort still seems to have interested Monte-verdi comparatively little. Admittedly the title of the next madrigal book is *Concerto. Settimo libro de madrigali a 1, 2, 3, 4 & 6 voci, con altri generi de canti*. We might expect now, only seventeen years after Caccini's *Nuove Musiche* appeared, to see Monteverdi's contribution to the history of monody. The contents reveal that we are likely to be disappointed. Only four out of over thirty works are for solo voice and only two of these are works for the simple combination of voice and keyboard. The other two demand some form of instrumental accom-paniment or intervention. The rest of these madrigals are duets, trios and *ensemble* music of various kinds, including the ballet *Tirsi et Clori*, which, as we shall see in a later chapter, belongs to the madrigalesque *genre* only in the way that some of the great choruses for plays which appeared in other composers' madrigal books throughout the sixteenth century did. The very shape of the book is most unusual, and although we can find a similar *mélange* in the work of another senior composer—Marco da Gagliano's *Musiche* (1615), which also contains monodies, duets and a *balletto*—even in this there is not quite the rich diversity of Monteverdi's set.

The works for solo voice are emotionally the least significant, although all are interesting in some way. The two most difficult for the twentieth-century musician to understand are the *lettere amorose*,

[1] Printed in W. Osthoff, *12 composizioni vocali . . . (inedite)*, Milan, 1958.

written in the *genere rappresentativo* (or recitative style) and designed to be sung in a free rhythm. These are 'academic' monodies of the most severe kind, and it is rather surprising to find that they are so different from the climaxes of the operas. More ingratiating is the first work in the volume, *Tempro la cetra*. This is an aria in the sense that the word had been used by the Florentines—a set of strophic variations. There are four verses to be set, and the bass part of each is kept roughly the same (there are minor changes of rhythm). Over this the singer develops his theme. He has taken the lyre to sing to the glory of Mars, but as the first verse ends, he declares that all he can sing of is love. Each verse contrasts the images of war and love and gives the singer the opportunity for varying the melody. In each verse he increases the expressiveness of the ornaments, until the last stanza brings forth the *trillo* and the whole repertory of *gorgie*. To offset this, Monteverdi provides a little *ritornello* for five unnamed instruments, in the manner of *Orfeo*. As it is repeated between the verses, it seems little more than a conventional device; and then, as it seems to be about to bring the piece to an end, Monteverdi adds a little dance which is given twice before the *ritornello* finally does end the piece. The work is obviously an offshoot of Orpheus' aria to Charon, although more simple in its decoration and less intense, more playful in mood.

The fourth solo work is unique. *Con che soavità* is written for a soprano accompanied by three groups of instruments. The first consists only of *continuo* instruments—two *chitarroni*, a harpsichord and a spinet; the second, two violins, viola and a harpsichord; the third, viola and cello (or two viols) and *contrabasso* with an organ. The conception is based on the dialogues which were so popular in both church music and chamber monody; but instead of a voice with each group of instruments Monteverdi gives the words to a single voice, which sings virtually continuously. As usual when he grafts a new idea on to old forms, his inspiration runs high. The comparatively slow-moving harmonies traditional in dialogues, to accommodate the large forces performing them, fit exactly the work's mood suggested by the word 'soavità' (sweetness) in the opening phrase. But then the passion of the lover's kisses comes to life suddenly and powerfully in the contrasts which can be conjured up with the three instrumental groups. The vocal melody, by using the repetitions which are so much part of the dialogue form, is magically organized, always *arioso* rather than recitative in its steady rhythms and tight phrase structure. There is no need for extravagant decoration or severe dissonance. As a result the piece is one of the most contented of love madrigals, never violent yet never frivolous. It is a pity it is not more widely known, though perhaps understandable since the resources needed for its performance are not easy to come by.

The most notable masterpieces of the book, however, are the duets. They take up about half the volume and several of them seem in their emotional richness to hark back to the greatness of Book IV. It is not surprising that Monteverdi took to the medium so well. As we have seen, much of his earlier work had used the duet texture for long stretches even though it retained the variety inherent in larger resources; and duets suited him better than pure monodic writing. Fullness of harmony and expanded forms came out of the duet more easily than from the solo. Monteverdi borrowed what he required from the monody, but these duets are essentially a development of his earlier quasi-contrapuntal style. This will be clearer if we compare his duets with some by Gagliano. There are several in Gagliano's *Musiche*, and they divide quite naturally into slightly built strophic songs and more serious and complicated *continuo* madrigals. The strophic songs are clearly ariettas, with a melody, a bass and the second voice filling in. Short phrases and regular harmonic changes give a pleasant tuneful-ness, and variety is worked in by the instrumental interludes, which, however, never break up the phrase structure and seem to belong to the melody of the voice. The serious duets are another matter. They are declamatory, use the *gorgia* for the normal monodic expressiveness and have slower moving harmony. Here again, there are repeated sections where the voices change parts as had been customary in canzonets and balletts for a long time.

To compare Gagliano's slighter duets with Monteverdi's *Chiome d'oro* is perhaps unfair since Monteverdi's work seems on a so much more extended scale; but the works are similar, and *Chiome d'oro* is really an extension of the style of the *Scherzi musicali*, which certainly are comparable. The idea of instrumental *ritornellos* has been taken from the *Scherzi musicali* and the actual form of the duet also reminds us of them for it is in essence a strophic song with everything repeated twice. But there are some important differences. The *ritornello* is quite a complicated piece with three closely related strains, and instead of using all of it between the sung verses, Monteverdi uses the strains separately in between various lines of the poem. The vocal melody itself is superb, using the dotted rhythms which had previously been ornaments so consistently that they became the whole spring-board of the tune. Typically for Monteverdi, though much of the time the voices sing in thirds with one another, they interchange occasionally and add little roulades which mean that both are entirely necessary and that the piece is thus a genuine duet. Typical too are the two little cadenzas, as they seem to be, at the end of each stanza—typical, for they insert into a song of flirtation a touch of deeper feeling, without ever being heavy or sentimental.

The more serious works explore the resources of the duet even more thoroughly. The one which at first sight seems nearest to monody is *Interrotte speranze*; and yet this is a work far away from Florence. It is a song of a spurned lover whose hope and faith merely raise his desire. It begins with a pedal note in the bass. Over this two tenors begin the plaint, chanting on the same note. In a way which Monteverdi had used in his earlier madrigals, dissonances are produced by the upper part moving up a tone and thrusting the lower part down. These dissonances and the rise in the melody, the sustained pedal note, the broken phrases, the low *tessitura* for the voices, all establish the psychology of the despairing, desiring lover in a very powerful way. And then, when the pedal note has changed and the cadence has provided relief, Monteverdi repeats all this nervous material, only with altered, even more intense declamation. This cannot be kept up, and the music relaxes with a dialogue and more sober thoughts about the beloved. Only at the end are the dissonances resumed to twist the knife in our hearts:

In this duet it is the declamatory opening with the static bass that gives the appearance of monody; and it is possible to find many similar places in the duets of this volume. The expressive ornamentation also seems 'monodic' at first sight, and so do the sudden changes of harmony. But in fact the real power of these emotionally rich works lies in their derivation from older sources. The scale is achieved essentially by the methods of the older madrigal books, that is by repeating sections of varying lengths with new tone colouring. In *Perchè fuggi*, for example, almost every melodic phrase is repeated— not with a sterile one-voice-after-the-other method, but by using the second voice in the repetitions to add new counterpoints, enriching the harmony and timbre. As for the ornamentation, it is less 'monodic', or based on the expression of a single word or phrase, than an integral part of the melody—a dotted rhythm repeated again and again to balance the phrase, or a *portamento* which comes in each voice in turn to become a memorable fragment to shape the melody (as in *Ecco vicine, o bella tigre*). This is nearer the continuous application of ornament which was so common in the sixteenth century, though, it must be said, with the application of much more purpose and skill than the improvising singers can ever have achieved. Out of virtuosity has come a rhythmical melody which can truly be called tuneful.

All these duets are fine, and they show a very wide emotional range. The flirtatious *Tornate, o cari baci* with its refrain of kisses, the richly decorated *O come sei gentile* for two virtuoso ladies or the more serious kisses of *Perchè fuggi* form a splendid treasure which is every bit as deserving of revival as the early polyphonic madrigals. All are reward-ing and only one of them can be mentioned as standing out from the rest—the set of variations on the *romanesca* theme, *Ohimè, dov'è il mio ben?* The idea is borrowed from the song-books, for the duet is a set of strophic variations. There are four sections, each with the same stock bass, over which two tenors sing the lament, 'Where has my beloved gone, who has robbed me?' The words remind us of the *Lamento d'Arianna*, and so does the music. The first section, with its short, stabbing phrases intensified with dissonance between the voices, has the same bitter agony. If anything, the agony is greater, as the imita-tions between the voices expand the scale and make pure declamation unnecessary by their overlapping rhythms. As in the earlier work, Monteverdi uses a refrain technique to make the music highly taut. The bass itself suggests this by a repeated cadential figure, but the repetitions in the melody are of greater length than those of the bass, and Monteverdi glories in the clashes which necessarily arise. Even more remarkable is the command of harmony which gives the piece its emotional variety. The final cadence in each successive verse expresses in turn despair, agony, the sweetness of hope and the finality of death:

It was another thirteen years before a new madrigal book of Monteverdi's appeared. They were years in which the nature of secular music changed completely. The serious monodic madrigals of the Florentine and Roman virtuosos went out of fashion, and a taste arose for the simpler, more obviously popular songs. Monteverdi's younger assistants at St Mark's were especially good at composing these. Berti and Grandi published some song-books in which tunefulness is all. Light rhythms, regular phrases, clear-cut diatonic harmonies became the order of the day. The verse was if anything even more trivial than the canzonet verse of the sixteenth century. In the more serious songs there are sometimes passages in the older declamatory style, but they often end with a gay triple-time section to provide easily memorable music (giving a division into recitative and aria, which became familiar later on). When more complicated music was required, it was usually given the form of the strophic variation, with the bass repeated in the manner of Caccini; or else an *ostinato* bass was employed. It is doubtful whether Monteverdi really cared very much for this frothy music, in which the academic theories of the earlier composers of monody had completely disappeared. Yet it was too important and popular for him to be able to ignore it. He contributed about half a dozen pieces to various Venetian anthologies; and the book of *Scherzi musicali* which came out in 1632 (significantly with a dedication by the publisher Magni, who clearly had gathered the collection together himself, a sign perhaps of Monteverdi's indifference) is in fact a book of arias in this new style.

The simplest of these songs are as near as Monteverdi ever went to writing in a purely conventional style. Catchy little tunes to insignificant verses, they have the charm of their *genre* but little individuality. The only way they can be said to differ from the works of many lesser composers is that Monteverdi can never resist the temptation to 'paint' the words, even if it breaks up the balance of phrases and the general mood of the song. A little chromatic passage to illustrate the word 'dying' or a succession of dissonances to express the cruelty of the lady intrude themselves. The strophic variation arias can accommodate these old-fashioned methods better, allowing for melodic variety in each verse, and Monteverdi usually adds a little *ritornello* for instruments in between, to give still more subtle emotional opportunities. *Et è pur dunque vero* is a good example of the style, the same bass allowing ample scope for melodic devices to express the weeping of the lover and the triumph and apparent indifference of the beloved, interspersed with a host of natural images such as the murmuring of the wind.

But as usual, Monteverdi's full inspiration is best found in *ensemble* music and especially in the duets, now clearly his favourite medium. The editor of one anthology, Anselmi, was very lucky to be given such a fine piece as *O come vaghi*. The poem is the conventional nonsense about Lydia and her eyes being wounding darts; but Monteverdi draws from it all its meaning and gives it a depth it scarcely deserves.

First there comes the rich sound of two tenors singing in thirds, and then as the lover is bewitched they split up, and in alert, lightly imitative phrases build up a climax. As the rays from Lydia's eyes become little arrows Monteverdi invents a motif which in pure sound, a dental consonant followed by a smooth vowel melisma, shoots out in a strikingly realistic way, multiplies in imitations between the voices and then, as the lover is wounded, is lost in dissonances. The harmonies become astringent as the pain increases:

Then quite suddenly the sweetness of love is felt, and with a motif reminiscent of the beginning of *O Mirtillo* a consonant and still section ends the duet, disturbed only by the cadential dissonance, as the 'dying' of the lover is mentioned in the poem. This is a subtle piece of erotic music, which, like some of the earlier madrigals from Book IV, is effortless in passing from flirtation to true love, from love's climax to perfect peace.

Madrigals with Basso Continuo

Of the other duets of this period, *Zefiro torna* is deservedly famous. The poem is not the usual one by Petrarch, which Monteverdi had set in Book VI. It is a sort of 'parody' (in the sixteenth-century sense) of it by Rinuccini and, most important, keeps the same contrast between joyful nature and the lover abandoned to his doleful thoughts. Monteverdi sets this as a chaconne, using an *ostinato* bass pattern very popular about this time:

The form is a difficult one. The shortness of the bass pattern (compared with others such as the *romanesca*) means short phrase lengths which can become tiresome, and the harmonies are not easily varied enough for an extended piece. Monteverdi conquers these problems magnificently. His first paragraph lasts a dozen bars, as each voice replies with a variant of the initial theme; and then the sweetness of the breeze, slightly syncopated, is expressed by a succession of pure consonances. There are gentle roulades for the murmuring waves, pictorial motifs for the valleys and mountains (complete with the echo device) in fact all the imagery of *Ecco mormorar l'onde* in the form of a duet. Then, as the lover speaks of his plight, a piece of recitative with dissonances is ushered in with a great chromatic change, brought to a peaceful end as the lover sings praise of his lady's eyes in an ornamental, sonorous passage with trills and scales in thirds. The technical mastery of the piece is astonishing. Out of conventional features—the *ostinato* bass, the by now customary division into speech-rhythm recitative and dance-rhythm aria, echo music and so on—Monteverdi builds up a vivid picture, and one which proves him to be a composer by no means *semper dolens*.

The remainder of his secular music appeared in three collections, an eighth book of madrigals (1638), the *Selva morale e spirituale* (1640) and a posthumous collection put out by Vincenti in 1651. It is impossible to date the individual numbers. All that can be certain is that they were composed over a considerable space of time, probably between about 1625 and 1635. Those of the trios which Vincenti put out in 1651 seem to belong in atmosphere to the lightest of the *Scherzi musicali*. They are gay dance songs with strong rhythms and tonalities typical of the trivia common in Venice around 1630. They are usually strophic songs, sometimes given a little variety by each of the three singers in turn having a little solo at the beginning of the verse, sometimes plainly repetitive. Most of them are either written completely or for a large part in triple time, although one or two divide into recitative and dance song as in so many arias of Berti, Merula and other minor composers of the time.

These works might make us believe that Monteverdi had surrendered the high ideals of music gained in the academies of his youth. He had certainly not followed blindly the ideas of the *camerata* composers and the 'advanced' madrigalists; but the old ideas were in his mind to the end. The eighth book of madrigals has a new title: *Madrigali guerrieri et amorosi*, not forgetting a preface which carefully explains the contents:

I have reflected that the principal passions or affections of our mind are three, namely, anger, moderation and humility or supplication; so the best philosophers declare, and the very nature of our voice indicates this in having high, low and middle registers. The art of music also points clearly to these three in its terms 'agitated', 'soft' and 'moderate' [*concitato, molle* and *temperato*]. In all the works of former composers I have indeed found examples of the 'soft' and the 'moderate', but never of the 'agitated', a genus nevertheless described by Plato in the third book of his *Rhetoric* [1] in these words: 'Take that harmony that would fittingly imitate the utterances and the accents of a brave man who is engaged in warfare.' And since I was aware that it is contraries which greatly move our mind, and that this is the purpose which all good music should have—as Boethius asserts, saying: 'Music is related to us and either ennobles or corrupts the character' —for this reason I have applied myself with no small diligence and toil to rediscover this genus.

After reflecting that according to all the best philosophers the fast pyrrhic measure was used for lively and warlike dances, and the slow spondaic

[1] Actually the *Republic*: the reference is 399*a*.

measure for their opposites, I considered the semibreve, and proposed that a single semibreve should correspond to one spondaic beat; when this was reduced to sixteen semiquavers struck one after the other and combined with words expressing anger and disdain, I recognized in this brief sample a resemblance to the passion which I sought, although the words did not follow metrically the rapidity of the instrument.

To obtain a better proof I took the divine Tasso as a poet who expresses with the greatest propriety and naturalness the qualities which he wishes to describe, and selected his description of the combat of Tancred and Clorinda as an opportunity of describing in music contrary passions, namely, warfare and entreaty and death. In the year 1624 I caused this composition to be performed in the noble house of my especial patron and indulgent protector the Most Illustrious and Excellent Signor Girolamo Mocenigo, an eminent dignitary in the service of the Most Serene Republic, and it was received by the best citizens of the noble city of Venice with much applause and praise. . . .

My rediscovery of this warlike genus has given me occasion to write certain madrigals which I have called *guerrieri*. And since the music played before great princes at their courts to please their delicate taste is of three kinds according to the method of performance—theatre music, chamber music and dance music—I have indicated these in my present work with the titles *guerriera, amorosa* and *rappresentativa*.[1]

If ever a madrigal book required some sort of explanation it is this one. It puzzles us today; it probably puzzled Monteverdi's contemporaries nearly as much. Instead of the usual chamber music for a few voices and instruments this one contains some big choral works and three dramatic ones (one, a ballet written thirty years earlier) as well as duets and trios. Then the arrangement into madrigals of war and those of love was unique. All madrigals (more or less) dealt with love: but what were warlike madrigals? No wonder the volume was never reprinted.

We might well dismiss the warlike part of the volume as speculative compositions to demonstrate a theory if it were not for two things.

[1] Translation taken from Strunk, *Source Readings in Music History* (London, 1952), pages 413–15.

One was that Monteverdi had always liked concrete imagery in the verse he set and managed to put it into realistic music. Then warlike music was not by any means new, although the audience of the 1620's and 1630's may not have remembered it. In the sixteenth century there had been a vogue of battle pieces, started by Jannequin's *La Bataille de Marignan*. By the second half of the century the vogue had reached Venice and two of the St Mark's musicians, Padovano and Andrea Gabrieli, wrote instrumental pieces called *arie della battaglia* for the Venetian wind band. Fanfares and military calls of various kinds were the stuff of this music, which was a form of elementary realism; and these pieces had an immense popularity in the 1590's. Monteverdi must have known them, but he would only use their methods after he had justified himself on theoretical grounds.

The works for a few voices from the 'warlike' part of the eighth book are the nearest to his normal style. One of them, *Armato il cor*, had been included by Magni in the *Scherzi musicali*, where it hardly seems out of place; and the other duet, *Se vittorie si belle*, also seems at first sight reasonably normal. Neither piece is a description of a battle. Both are settings of love poems with conventional warlike metaphors (as had been *Non più guerra* in Book IV); and both have the natural division between a fight and possible victory, and defeat and the wounds of death. There is no novelty in this, and seemingly not much in the music with its extended triple-time passages and contrasting, less rhythmic sections; and if there is some realistic musical imagery, this is, as we have seen, quite normal for Monteverdi.

Nevertheless there are differences. The warlike sections, built up from melodic fanfare arpeggios, are much simpler than anything we find in such duets as *Interrotte speranze* and *Tornate*. The harmonies are almost completely consonant and huge sections use two and three common chords, tonic and dominant predominating. Syncopations are rare, the rhythms being very straightforward and dance-like. The supposedly contrasting sections, where victory is in doubt and the poet is preoccupied with love's wounds, are equally unusual. Instead of the normal dissonances, Monteverdi maintains a remarkably pure harmony (again full of sequences and other devices which emphasize a diatonic key structure). *Se vittorie si belle* ends with a peaceful passage which completely ignores the implication of 'morir' (death):

The result is curiously new. These works are completely Monteverdian, with all the old skills of creating a live, large-scale music which closely follows the sense of the words, but it is Monteverdi without the eroticism of his earlier works. In action or calmness, the works are extrovert, the images of the verse accepted at their face value rather than intensified as symbols of the lover's inner feelings.

Much the same may be said about the madrigals for six or more voices and instruments, although here the interest is often intensified by the splendid sonorities which are possible with a large group. *Ardo, avvampo*, for example, builds up a tremendous power in its first section, starting with two tenors, then adding two sopranos and finally four more voices and two violins. The first twenty-seven bars are simple repetitions of the G major chord, and the rest of this section is built from the simplest harmonic and melodic material. In *Altri canti d'amor* a similar effect is used in a big choral section, the fanfare material again well to the fore. These passages are thrilling, and yet the total effect of the madrigals is a little disappointing. They are too loosely organized, unlike Monteverdi's earlier *continuo* madrigals. It is customary to call them cantatas rather than madrigals, which means that they are sectional in construction. *Altri canti d'amor*, for example, has an overture, a trio, a central chorus, a bass solo accompanied by strings and a final chorus, all reasonably independent, though the final section grows out of the bass aria. The basic idea behind this kind of work came from the *concertato* motet, and like many of these it has too little sense of unity and climax for the form to be entirely satisfactory. The sections are not in themselves complete or well enough organized to stand as entities, but they seem to have distracted the composer from a satisfying overall construction. The problem is exactly the same one that Monteverdi had failed to solve completely in his first madrigal book. Clearly it took him a little time to gain the necessary experience with a new form.

The most successful piece in this style is one which approaches his earlier madrigals. *Hor che 'l ciel e la terra* is a setting of a poem by Petrarch, a sonnet which Monteverdi might have set at any time in his life. The lover cannot sleep, although heaven, earth and the wind are all silent. But his mind is at war within itself and only the thought of his beloved can bring peace. The image of war is only incidental to the theme, and so it appears in the music. The madrigal opens with a *parlando* section expressing the stillness of nature, very like those in the madrigals of Wert which had influenced Monteverdi in his youth. The colour of the voices—low in range—gives a magical, dark touch; and suddenly from this comes the dissonant, strident, curt lover's plaint, intensified in a duet for tenors. This is again very much in Monteverdi's older vein, and the only sign of the *stile concitato* comes in the passage actually setting the word 'guerra'. The passage is transient and gives way to a homophony expressive of the lover's peace while thinking about his lady. The madrigal which forms the second part of the setting is even more old-fashioned. For long passages the *basso continuo* could be removed and the harmony would remain complete. The eroticism is back, too, with chromatic scales imitated throughout the parts and declamatory sections repeated again and again to give the meaning to the words 'and thousands and thousands of times in a day I die and then am reborn'.

Hor che 'l ciel e la terra is successful because it really belongs to the *canti amorosi*, and in fact it is the second part of the eighth book that contains the most rewarding works. The madrigals for five or more voices are, as in the first part, less emotionally rich than the duets and trios, but they have a charm of their own. The two pieces marked *alla francese* are especially fresh, and *Dolcissimo uscignolo* is very effective, a charming melody given strength by the firm organization of alternating solo and *tutti* passages; and with some episodes tending towards the minor there is a touch of wistfulness which adds flavour to an otherwise contented and sweet-sounding piece. The same thing can be said of *Vago augelletto*, in which a small group of strings is added to the seven voices. The solo-tutti relationship is kept up and turned into a rondo form, and although there are some symbolic and more passionate bars for the words 'to pass the time in weeping', the same anacreontic spirit permeates the music.

The more intimate pieces—duets, trios and one quartet—are very different, and it is in these that Monteverdi's madrigalian art reaches its second climax. The trios are the lightest of the music—triple-time dance songs in the manner of a Venetian arietta but very deliberately handled and among the best of the *genre*. *Ninfa che scalza il piede* is a splendid example. One tenor first sings an arietta, with happy, regular rhythm organized into short repetitive motifs that remind us of *Tirsi e Clori*. A second tenor joins in for a new section as the lovers come together: and a touch of syncopation livens up the dance. Finally a bass is introduced and the dance continues, made more exciting by the gentle imitations in which the parts tumble one after another. And then, without interrupting the triple rhythm, a typically Monteverdian touch, the voices turn to the minor to exclaim, 'Ah, what a heart of stone', and with a dissonance here and there one voice or another anticipates the harmonies of the others.

The trios show one side of Monteverdi's musical character, the duets are equally typical of others. One of them, *Mentre vaga Angioletta*, is a setting of a poem in praise of music and gives the composer every chance of showing off the clever external manner well known from *Zefiro torna*. 'Murmuring', 'alternating flights', 'broken accents' —one can imagine Monteverdi's delight in these opportunities for tone painting. He takes them all and gives the voices their opportunities in richly ornamented lines. The most deeply felt duets, on the other hand, are two which are shorter and in the erotic tradition. *Ardo* and *O sia tranquillo il mare* are such fine works that it is not surprising that Vincenti printed them again in his volume of 1651. *Ardo* is in the tradition of *O come vaghi* and *Interrotte speranze*. 'I burn', cries the poet, 'but I burn more since I dare not tell of my passion.' Monteverdi sets this with an expansive gesture, the harmonies remaining on the chord of D minor as the voices rise to an immediate climax. They die away in dissonance (as usual arrived at by separating the voices in an imitative section) as courage fails:

The poet dares to call for help and the music surges to the upper register of the voices. It is useless, for when he is with his lady he would like to speak (a repeated fragment which breaks off suddenly) and dare not. He only trembles, and as he starts to tell of his love the words are broken on his lips:

There is realism in this madrigal, but it is an inner psychological reality, an expansion of the verbal imagery made vivid especially by the sudden changes of vocal range, the growth and breaking off of the melody. *O sia tranquillo il mare* is cast in the same emotional mould, although its technique is different. The poet never leaves the cliff top, whether the sea is calm or troubled, as he laments the loss of his beloved; but Phyllis never returns, and his laments and prayers are carried away on the wind. Monteverdi, again following the Venetian aria composers, divides the piece into a recitative followed by a triple-time aria. The recitative (not perhaps a truly accurate description of it since it is always rhythmic; but it is declamatory) sets the scene: calm chords for the tranquil sea, dissonance for the lament, a cry of agony as he weeps; then the aria, not a gay dance as so often in these triple-time pieces, rather a lost bewailing in the words, 'You do not return, my Phyllis, oh, you do not return', which are repeated again and again—sometimes in a continuous flowing melody, sometimes broken short and left to suggest mere exhaustion.

These duets are masterpieces, and there is one more great work in the book. This is the *Lamento della ninfa*, written for a soprano and three male voices. Monteverdi calls it a work in the *stile rappresentativo* or theatre style, but it needs no acting, any more than did the madrigal comedies of earlier years. The men tell us the story. A nymph is lamenting outside her dwelling the loss of her lover. They are objective, though sympathetic, and their music is there only to prepare for the second stage, the nymph's lament. This is a piece which defies description or quotation. It is a chaconne with a short bass pattern repeated thirty-four times. Over this the nymph cries out against her fate and the lover who has deserted her. Sometimes the men commiserate with her, one by one, or all together. They never join in her song, which is too heartfelt for anyone but her. At the end she is left by herself. Always the bass figure goes on as before, reminding her and us that her fate is eternal and that she will always be alone. There is dissonance and marvellously expressive melody, the more passionate because it is in the triple time of the dance measure, while always avoiding the strong accents of the aria, and Monteverdi tells the singer to sing it not in strict time but 'according to the mood'. None of these devices is in itself remarkable but together they make the piece unforgettable; and when the epilogue is sung by the men in the same objective style as the prologue, the contrast is sharp, the lament being made almost unbearably intense.

The eighth book is a worthy end to the series. Like the other volumes, it is never purely fashionable, nor artificially difficult or experimental. It is impossible to discuss the madrigal as a single form, for Monteverdi managed to adapt it to a variety of purposes; and it is not very helpful to call these later works cantatas, as though they were quite different from the earlier music. It is equally unsatisfactory to assume that Monteverdi's development is in fact the development of all music over the half-century. There is one principle which informs all Monteverdi's madrigals. He would have called it 'imitation'. We may call it fidelity to the truth of the poetry. Taught him in the academies of Mantua, he never forgot it, even when his younger contemporaries bothered about it very little. It made him take the madrigal seriously to the end of his life, even in the lightest of canzonets and arias. In the madrigal there was freedom to choose the verse which music could enhance, to give an even greater variety than was possible in opera, much less in church music. For his madrigals Monteverdi deserves a proud title: a great humanist.

CHAPTER VI

THE DRAMATIC MUSIC

OPERA was very new in 1607. *Orfeo* was to be the sixth *dramma per musica* ever written. To Monteverdi the form was even newer. He may have seen one of the Florentine operas, or he may have studied one of the scores—that was all. But if opera was new, dramatic music was not; plays with music were extremely common, especially in the free courts of northern Italy. Mantua was famed for its players, Ferrara and Venice for their court entertainments. The fashionable plays at these courts by the early years of the seventeenth century were the pastorals. To the Englishman the pastoral idiom is best known through the lyric poetry of *Comus* and *Lycidas*; or in the dramatic form in *As You Like It*, where Shakespeare gently pokes fun at its conventions. The scene is always an idealized countryside, the characters are shepherds and shepherdesses. The main subject-matter is love, at first frustrated by circumstance but eventually brought to a happy ending. The shepherdess Sylvia refuses to love the shepherd Amyntas who loves her. At the climax of the play Sylvia will be reported dead, killed by a wolf, or in some other accident. Amyntas, given this news by a messenger, will despair and go away to commit suicide; whereupon Sylvia will reappear and realize on hearing of her lover's fate that she really loves him. Finally, Amyntas will come back, having failed to kill himself, and the pair will be happily united. Add to this a host of confidants, some gods and goddesses to speak a prologue and intervene at vital moments, and we have the recipe for the pastoral play.

Taken as drama the pastoral is usually far too slow and often preposterous. It is quite impossible to believe in these idealized shepherds who speak in beautiful lyrical verse and whose main interest is to convey hopeless passion at some length. When Shake-speare borrowed the pastoral idea he took care to insert some real yokels, who at least have some action in them. But such criticisms are rather beside the point. The pastorals were not considered purely as drama, and in reading them today we have only the bare bones of the entertainment. Its flesh was ornate scenery, machines and a great deal of elaborate music. The spectacle was especially important, and no expense was spared. Today it is difficult to imagine the splendour of the scene. How can we re-create in our minds the wonder and delight of the audience when they saw 'a vast and most lovely canvas painted with various animals hunted and taken in divers ways, which, upheld by a great cornice and concealing the prospect scene' took up the whole of one end of a great hall? Or their amazement at the perspective scenes in which the woods and fields seemed to stretch back to the distant horizon? Or the gorgeousness of the machines—clouds which opened to reveal gods and goddesses in the sky and which moved high across the stage?

The music for these pastorals was almost as splendid. We never possess it in its entirety, for full scores were unknown, but some of the numbers appeared in the madrigal books. The choruses, in which the voices were joined by instrumental *ensembles*, must have sounded magnificent. There were solo songs and some dances—as we know from one stage designer who insisted that the stage must be made solid enough to take the strain of the energetic *morescas*.[1] And as if this spectacle in the play were not enough, there were the intermezzos which came during the intervals and at the end of the play itself. The intermezzos had little dramatic action and their whole interest lay in the scenic designs and the machines. The gods here came into their own, and their cloud machines were ornate beyond belief. Infernal scenes where smoke and fire effects could be used were quite common. The allegorical figures of Hope and Fear and so on were carried on the stage in floats, splendidly decorated to illustrate the theme.

[1] For further descriptions see L. C. Campbell, *Scenes and Machines on the English Stage during the Renaissance* (Cambridge, 1923).

Speech was less important than songs, for there was no action to be made clear. The orchestra was often large—forty players were not uncommon—and it was used dramatically. Trombones for infernal scenes, recorders for the zephyrs, and similar effects, were the stock-in-trade of the composer. Here too there were large-scale choruses and elaborate dances. Such magnificence was bound to take up the energies of composers, not to mention the attention of the audience. 'Once', said one playwright ruefully, 'we used to have intermezzos to serve the plays. Now we have plays to serve as excuses for intermezzos.' Someone interested mainly in drama could have said much the same about the French court ballet at the time. Here again there was some dramatic action completely swamped by the interest in the spectacle. Naturally dances were of the first importance, but both drama and music had to be subordinated to the demands of the eye.

Monteverdi knew all these *genres* well; he was to write music for every one of them by the end of his life. But before his *Orfeo* came into existence there were the other five operas to make possible a drama set in continuous music. It is easy to see why the Florentine composers and theorists were dissatisfied with dramatic music in its conventional form. The plays with music mixed up with the intermezzos and the French court ballet were essentially distracted by spectacle from their principal aim—a truly dramatic action. It is also easy to see why they used recitative, for though it is true that they misinterpreted the ideas of the Greeks, their instinct was sound. If the full power of music was given only to the static moments of the play, interest would naturally concentrate there, and the conflict of action which is the basis of drama would inevitably be lost.

To regain a sense of drama in the new form the Florentines took to a process of simplification. In place of the complications of the pastoral play, with its sub-plots and large casts, they set the simple story of Orpheus and Eurydice to music. Admittedly they retained the pastoral idiom with a great deal of lyricism and the conventional happy ending. Orpheus finds his wife in Hades and thereafter there is no complication of losing her again. There is a prologue by an allegorical figure, Tragedy, which as we have seen was a common feature of the pastoral plays; and a messenger scene when the news of Eurydice's death is given is equally conventional. Some of the songs and choruses must also have seemed quite normal to the Florentine audience. Two features, on the other hand, are new. There is no sign of important orchestral music or the large number of instrumentalists assembled for the plays and intermezzos. Most important of all is the recitative in which the story is carried on.

The Florentine recitative has been much maligned. It has admittedly little variety of phrase length, since the composers nearly always stop at the end of each line of verse with a cadence. Even so, some of it is highly expressive and in the hands of intelligent singers and actors must have had an excellent effect. A juster criticism is that the composers seem to have had little conception of musical form on a broader scale. Believing that the drama must be left to do its own work they made no attempt to build up climaxes in musical terms. There can have been little in the music that the audience found really memorable, and none of the effects which can be brought about by organizing the music into the repetitive forms which give it its great emotional possibilities. In parts the audience may well have been deeply moved by the total effect of acting and music, but it is difficult to believe that it was continuously interested.

Given this background and Monteverdi's gift for intelligent borrowing, the form and manner of his new opera were almost predictable. Striggio, the librettist, must have known the poet Guarini, the most famous writer of pastorals, quite well, and the idiom of pastoral verse was second nature to him. In borrowing the idea of the Orpheus story in a pastoral version from the Florentines there may have been more than a small element of rivalry. What is interesting is that Striggio retained much more of the dramatic flavour in the story than Rinuccini had done.

First there is a prologue, sung by an allegorical figure, Music. The first act and a half are taken up with the rejoicing of shepherds and shepherdesses, including the hero and the heroine. This is purely in the pastoral lyrical tradition, and so is the first element of drama, the arrival of the messenger bearing the news of Eurydice's death.

Orpheus' reaction is again in terms of pastoral, a lyrical despair from which he emerges only slowly when he resolves to seek her in Hades. The beginning of Act III introduces another allegorical figure, Hope, who seems to have been brought in from an intermezzo, and Orpheus is led to the banks of the River Styx. There he is given an opportunity to persuade Charon to ferry him across to Hades. Charon eventually goes to sleep and Orpheus crosses the Styx. In the next act we see Orpheus in Hades. After a discussion between Pluto and Proserpina he is allowed to return to earth with his wife.

At this point Striggio, instead of surrendering the drama of the story as the Florentines had done, continues with it, in spite of the difficulty of ending it in the pastoral tradition. Orpheus must not look back on his journey; but 'though Pluto forbids it, Love commands it', sings Orpheus. He looks behind him at Eurydice and his beloved wife is claimed by death. The final act presented Striggio with a problem. A pastoral had a happy ending, the Greek story its inevitable, tragic one. Striggio instinctively preferred the strength of the original to the watered-down tragi-comedy dénouement. His first version (as we learn from the printed libretto of 1607) begins the fifth act with Orpheus in the fields of Thrace, singing a song which is echoed from a rock. This is again pure pastoral; Guarini has a splendid echo scene in *Il pastor fido*. After this, Striggio leaves the pastoral convention and becomes a purist. The Bacchants enter, and with solo and choruses bring the play to its macabre end. This, however, was too strong for Monteverdi.[1] Orpheus' echoed lament in the fields was just what he wanted. But after that he took the easier course and either wrote himself, or made Striggio write, a happy ending. The god Apollo takes pity on Orpheus and descending on a cloud takes him up to heaven, to the satisfaction of the chorus.

If this ending seems to us unsatisfactory we must remember that it

[1] What precisely happened between composer and librettist is unknown; but the situation is very reminiscent of that between Varesco and Mozart over *Idomeneo*. There the composer's emendations were sung, but the librettist's original verses were printed, so that the honour of both should be satisfied.

was no more preposterous than the ending of Tasso's pastoral *Aminta*, whose hero, having thrown himself over a cliff, has his fall most luckily broken half way down. Further, the last thing which the audience of a play usually saw was not the final act of the play itself, but the allegorical intermezzo which followed it. The new ending of *Orfeo* is clearly an intermezzo with the stage designer finding good use for his cloud machine. Indeed the whole opera libretto is a mixture of intermezzo and pastoral. The first two acts and the first half of the last one are completely pastoral. The prologue, the infernal scenes and the dénouement are intermezzos, all of them with splendid scenic opportunities. It is Striggio's achievement that the drama is still remarkably unified and in the third and fourth acts comes to a dramatic climax.

It is Monteverdi's achievement too, for he also welds the diverse musical elements which were suggested by Striggio's play into a unified structure. The first sign that he imagines opera in terms of the intermezzo and pastoral comes in the overture, a 'toccata' to be played on the complete orchestra. The orchestra is a large one, having fifteen string players, about a dozen brass and wind, and nine *continuo* instruments—harpsichords, a harp, lutes, organs, and a regal or reed organ. The strings are violins, violas and cellos (though there are bass viols and a contrabass viol as well), and two players have to be prepared to double on little violins (tuned an octave higher than those used today). The toccata must have sounded well, even though it is really a conventional flourish on a single chord.

When the curtain goes up to reveal the figure of Music (probably seated on some marvellously elaborate float) we hear Monteverdi's conception of monody. He uses not the pure recitative style of the Florentine operas but the *arioso* of the song-books such as Caccini's *Nuove Musiche*. Music's song is in fact an aria (in the monodist's sense), a set of strophic variations, the bass kept mainly the same for each verse while the voice varies the melody over it. The vocal melody is comparatively plain and gives its effects by different phrase-lengths and some 'affective' leaps which remind us of Monteverdi's madrigals. Intervening between each verse is a *ritornello*, a short instrumental piece rather like a pavane, to give a rondo form. There is nothing amorphous here. The music is as tightly organized as it can be, and could be played as a separate piece (it is very like *Tempro la cetra* in the seventh book of madrigals).

The prologue, on the other hand, is no test of the dramatic composer. The play itself is another matter. From the beginning of the first act we can see Monteverdi's strong desire for musical variety and form. A shepherd sets the scene with some recitative. His role is narrative and he cannot be allowed a full *continuo* madrigal. Nevertheless his recitative is well organized, and two phrases catch our attention with their brevity and isolation by rests:

When Monteverdi repeats his opening section to make a miniature *da capo* aria, it is these fragments that concentrate our attention on his formal pattern.

Then, broken only by short pieces of recitative, the shepherds' rejoicing is expressed in choruses. These are delightful. One could hardly have supposed Monteverdi capable of such charm and light-heartedness; for there is nothing like these lyrical dance songs in the madrigal-books. They are real canzonets, and are ornamental with a splendid lightness of touch which beats Gastoldi on his own ground.

Orpheus breaks into them with an *arioso*—a hymn to the sun. Again there is the same feeling of organization brought about, not this time by refrains, but by a balance of phrases, a similarity of rhythms and a large leap downwards to end each section. Then, to create the larger entity, Monteverdi repeats the choruses in the reverse order. As a coda he writes a chamber aria, setting three verses, one as a duet, the next as a trio and then a duet again, the bass each time kept roughly the same, with the melodies enriched by ornaments and a masterly variety of texture. And since the audience may not recognize the unity given by the bass, a *ritornello* again separates the verses to complete yet another rondo. The act ends with another chorus.

This act, lyrical in style and using established forms, must have been the easiest to write. The second act is much harder. The arrival of the messenger breaks the lyricism and demands a complete change of mood. The first part of it continues with the shepherds' rejoicing in the same manner as before; but it is clear that some climax must be brought about, if only to strengthen the contrast with the arrival of the tragic news. Monteverdi chooses an essentially modern means to bring it about—an aria. It is an aria in both the seventeenth-century and our modern sense of the word—a strophic song with a clear-cut melody, a strong rhythm and moving bass part to provide harmonic change. It is a *hemiolia* song, in much the same style as the *Scherzi musicali* of 1607, and like them provided with a *ritornello*. It has a splendid tune and could stand by itself as music; but, like all the best operatic music, it achieves its full significance only in its context. There is just time for a shepherd to praise the song and then the fateful messenger arrives.

Recitative is inevitable, for the messenger's news is narrative and must be understood; yet there is no loss of expressive power, rather the contrary. Monteverdi writes in a style quite different from that of the recitatives earlier in the opera. He reverts to the harmonic language of his madrigals and to the dissonance which seems to arise from a conflict between the movement of the upper part and the tardiness of the bass and its harmonies. Here his deliberate awkwardness of melody is at its finest:

The development of the scene follows the practice of Greek tragedy. The messenger at first tells the shepherds only of disaster, not of its nature. It is a shepherd who first asks her meaning. The messenger still tells only of sorrow. Orpheus himself asks her more sharply what she means. Only then in shorter and shorter phrases does she tell that Eurydice is dead. This is real musical dialogue, and the music with its curt sections and its changes of harmony as the messenger and Orpheus converse has the authentic accents of tragedy. The details of the messenger's story inevitably form a little of an anticlimax, for Monteverdi is preparing for Orpheus' own expression of grief. The description of Eurydice's death, crying 'Orfeo, Orfeo', makes one of the shepherds break out with the theme 'Ahi caso acerbo' with which the messenger had entered—a masterly touch. Orpheus' cry of despair comes in an *arioso* which ends with the helpless realization of his fate:

The dramatic action is now cast aside, and pastoral returns. The chorus of shepherds begin an elaborate *continuo* madrigal, in form like those of Book V, with duets and solos held together by a refrain for the full choir; and as a final stroke of genius, Monteverdi uses the messenger's entry theme as the bass of the refrain. Finally, the *ritornello* of the prologue returns to give the only hint that all may yet be saved.

This superb act is a remarkable achievement, the more so since so much of it had to be written in recitative and still had to avoid a lack of tension. The act which follows was so like an intermezzo in Striggio's libretto that Monteverdi probably found it more familiar. The figure of Hope leading Orpheus, the arrival at the Styx (with a boat to be pulled across) and the infernal chorus to end the scene, all offer the producer opportunities, so that such recitative as is necessary need not be so emotionally charged (though again it is well organized with refrains and never seems amorphous). The difficult moment must have been the song in which Orpheus used all the powers of music to persuade the boatman to ferry him across. Again Monteverdi uses a solo chamber aria with several verses held together by the same bass and separated from one another by instrumental interludes. With sure insight he starts his song with a virtuoso strophe, full of opulent ornamentation; and then finding the boatman still unyielding, tries even harder in a second and then a third verse, each richer in ornament than the last. This compels admiration, not pity; and as if realizing this, Orpheus sings a simpler and more natural melody, till his plea becomes a pathetic *arioso*. This in itself would be moving. The instrumental interludes make it more so. First violins, then cornetts, and then a *ritornello* from the harp reinforce the plea, until, in keeping with the general plan, the virtuosity of the soloist gives way to a small string *ensemble* which plays simple echoes of the voice.

The infernal scenes which take up the second part of this act and all the succeeding ones are musically less splendid, though with the smoke and fire of hell which the producer must have provided the total effect was probably impressive enough.[1] There is a lilting song for

[1] There is a close analogy between this scene and one of the intermezzos given during the celebrations of the wedding of the Prince of Tuscany

Orpheus to sing as he reclaims his beloved Eurydice and a very dramatic recitative when he fails to conquer his desire to see her again. The last act is less of a dramatic entity, but, as we have seen, an audience used to intermezzos would scarcely have noticed this. The first part is an echo song—a fashionable device of which scores were written in the years round 1600, but none the worse for that. Then, after Orpheus' *arioso* has reached its climax, a short instrumental piece allows Apollo to descend on a cloud machine, and the pair ascend to heaven singing an ornamental duet. A chorus and dancing (the inevitable *moresca*) end the evening's entertainment.

Orfeo has been called the first real opera, and with justice; for it was not an experimental work or the result of theorizing, as the Florentine operas had been. At the same time in using the term 'opera' there are dangers that we may expect the interests of later opera composers to be Monteverdi's also. He clearly made little attempt to produce a set of characters seen in the round, as Mozart did, or to provide vivid dramatic action. His interest was more in a series of moods, in setting poetry in a lyrical rather than a dramatic way and in preserving a basic unity of musical forms.

The score of his second opera, *Arianna*, is lost,[1] although the libretto and several versions of its greatest scene have been preserved. From Rinuccini's poem we can see the way opera was to change. He was still working in the medium of pastoral, and the prologue and the final scene, where Ariadne joins the gods as the wife of Dionysus, are pure intermezzo. Even so, there seems to be much more emphasis on the

---

described by Vasari (*Vite de' pittori*, page 340). Four horrible serpents came on the stage to the accompaniment of trombones and *violons* (double bass viols) and with smoke and fire which came from an opening in the ground. Cerberus with three heads and other monsters were seen, and finally Charon with his boat, into which the desperate Psyche entered together with Envy, Jealousy, Thought and Scorn. Similar examples can be found in other intermezzos, e.g. in the description of the marriage celebrations of Piriteo Malvezzi and Beatrice Orsina in Bologna in 1585.

[1] For a full synopsis of the plot see J. A. Westrup, 'Monteverdi's *Lamento d'Arianna*' in *Music Review*, i (1940), pages 146–7.

human beings, especially Ariadne herself. Her lament is one of Monteverdi's most moving compositions. Originally it was a solo interrupted by a chorus of fishermen, who moralize on the theme of her sadness, and again it seems likely to have been an offshoot of the *continuo* madrigals in the style of those in Book V. The recitative-arioso (which is all we have left) is clearly written in the style of the greatest moments of *Orfeo*, with strong dissonances arising between voice and harmony instruments, 'affective' intervals and refrains. Monteverdi had no compunction about repeating words, and right from the start he uses this to create balanced phrases and a natural development of the melody as melody (not just as declamation), which makes the first section of the lament, at least, unforgettable:

La - scia - te mi mo - ri - re, la - scia - te mi mo - ri - re.

The loss of *Arianna* is irreparable, not merely for the historian but for music itself. The *Ballo delle ingrate* written at the same time is not consistently good, but its moments of beauty are intense enough to make us regret the loss of any music which Monteverdi wrote in this fecund time of 1608. It is an interesting work, the more so because it gives us some idea of the roots of *Orfeo*, since it is a ballet in the French style, a form known to Monteverdi perhaps since 1598. The scene, the jaws of hell, grimly lit with internal fire, is similar to that of Acts III and IV of *Orfeo*. The opening action of the ballet is a dialogue between Venus and Amor, in which Amor asks Venus to plead with Pluto to allow the *ingrate* (women who have preserved hard hearts against their lovers) to come up to earth. The resemblance to *Orfeo* becomes still more pronounced when Pluto eventually allows the *ingrate* to come to earth, to warn the ladies of the audience against a similar fate. The dialogue recitative during this part of the ballet is more interesting than moving, in spite of an attractive little *continuo* madrigal with *ritornellos* sung by Venus, and some very effective *arioso* using the deep register of Pluto's voice.

Then, quite suddenly, Monteverdi's inspiration returns. As the *ingrate* come from the fires of Hades, even Amor (whose reason for wishing to see them had been the malicious desire to gloat over them) is moved to pity, and in a short but moving duet Amor and Venus express their horror at the fate of these unloving ones. Dances in the French style ensue and at the end of them Pluto points the moral in a long *arioso* with a recurring instrumental interlude. Then, as he bids the *ingrate* return to Hades, one of the unfortunates sings a final lament, as pathetic and as powerful as Ariadne's. The ladies of the fashionable audience were moved to tears, and no wonder. For the 'cruel fate' which is so wonderfully expressed in Monteverdi's dissonant and broken *arioso* is given added point as he contrasts it with the consonance and smoothness and simplicity of the 'serene and pure air' which now the *ingrate* must leave behind for ever:

This marvellous scene would probably have been lost with so much of Monteverdi's dramatic music if he had not in a mood of reminiscence included the whole *ballo* in his eighth madrigal book in 1638.

The next piece of music for the stage also survived in a madrigal book. This was the ballet *Tirsi e Clori*, written for Mantua in 1615. It is music for the stage—but hardly dramatic music, for it is purely dance song with the minimum of action. It begins with a dialogue, with Thyrsis trying to persuade Chloris to dance and Chloris resisting him. Thyrsis sings in a gay dance measure, his beloved replies in a less exuberant *arioso* and a chorus of shepherds combine with a small group of strings in a series of dances. It is a charming piece but not one of the first importance, significant mainly because it shows Monteverdi's lessening interest in recitative and his growing control of the light aria style which replaced the new music with still newer music in Venice.

In the succeeding ten years Monteverdi wrote a number of dramatic works, none of which exists today. In 1616 he was composing a *favola marittima*—in no way different from a pastoral except that it was to be performed on the water, perhaps on the Mincio at Mantua. The correspondence about this is fascinating. Monteverdi obviously believed when he received the libretto that it was to be an opera 'sung and represented in music as was *Arianna*'. From this point of view the poem was highly unsatisfactory, and in one striking passage we gain a good idea of his approach to the aesthetics of opera:

I have observed that the personages of the drama are winds, *amoretti*, *zeffiretti* and sirens, so that we shall need many sopranos: moreover that the winds—the west winds and the north winds—have to sing. How, dear sir, shall I be able to imitate the speech of the winds since they do not speak? And how shall I be able to move the passions by their means? Ariadne moved the audience because she was a woman, and equally Orpheus because he was a man and not a wind. [Musical] sounds can imitate sounds —the rushing of winds, the bleating of sheep, the neighing of horses and so on—only without using words; but they cannot imitate the speech of the winds which does not exist . . . This tale, taken all in all, does not move my feelings in the least, due perhaps to my no little ignorance, and I find it difficult to understand, nor does it inspire me to a moving climax. *Arianna* inspired in me a true lament and *Orfeo* a true supplication; but as for this libretto, I do not know what it will inspire in me.[1]

This serious view of opera is confirmed in subsequent letters, for when Monteverdi was told by Striggio that this 'maritime tale' was really a series of intermezzos he settled down to write it, and bothered only about severely practical details, though it is significant that he never finished it. But it is clear that for him opera involved certain

[1] Malipiero, op. cit., page 166.

principles. Intermezzos were much less important, for they did not involve characterization in the same way. And the demand for an inspired climax—some set piece which will act as a focal point—shows that he understood the nature of opera far better than most of his contemporaries.

The letters on the abortive *Andromeda* and the eclogue on Apollo reveal more about Monteverdi's character than about his thinking on opera; and the fragment of music for the sacred drama *La Maddalena* is also unimportant. The next work, however, we possess in its entirety, and although it is unique in form, neither opera nor intermezzo, it is of the utmost importance in his development. This is *Il combattimento di Tancredi e Clorinda* (the fight of Tancred and Clorinda), which was produced in Girolamo Mocenigo's palace in 1624 and published in the eighth book of madrigals. In the madrigal book Monteverdi tells us that it was intended to be performed during a musical evening after madrigals had been sung in the normal way, without any scenery or action to distract the eye. Clearly then, *Il combattimento* was not meant to be like any of the other music for the stage. It demands a small orchestra of strings and only three voices. The poem was not a specially written libretto, but part of Tasso's *Gerusalemme liberata*, a description of a fight between Clorinda, who disguised as a man assaults the Christian encampment, and Tancred, a crusader, with whom, finding herself cut off, she fights in single combat. Having mortally wounded her, Tancred unlooses her armour and finds that his adversary is a woman. He is stricken with grief as she dies.

The difficulty of making the piece a success as a dramatic scene lies largely in the inhibiting necessity for a narrator who is rather more important than the two characters. The attraction, on the other hand, was the great one of demonstrating the new *stile concitato*. The result is that the voice parts are comparatively inexpressive, except for the final part of the work where Clorinda dies and where the recitative blossoms forth in the way we expect from Monteverdi at moments of climax. Elsewhere the interest is in the realistic sounds of battle—fanfares, clashing of swords and Tancred's horse galloping on to the scene—rendered by all the tricks of the trade such as pizzicatos, tremolandi,

sudden changes from loud to soft. For these tricks alone it is an interesting work; and for the biographer it is more so, as it reveals Monteverdi's tendency to realism which we have noticed in his letters about
the *favola marittima* above (not an uncommon feature of opera composers). But in itself *Il combattimento* is not entirely a success, as the
sympathy for its characters is rarely imparted to the audience. As a
form, this kind of dramatic scene is a dead end—but Monteverdi, as
so often, used the experience gained to good advantage in another
context.

No music at all has survived of the various pageants for Mantua and
Parma in which Monteverdi was engaged during the later 1620's.
Our most important loss is undoubtedly the opera, *Licori finta pazza*;
and since we have no trace even of Strozzi's libretto, it is difficult
to know precisely the sort of problem which faced the composer.
From his letters, however, we can see how his interests were developing. First, he was still trying out a theory of the affections and was
trying to divide the human emotions in the way which we find
in the eighth book of madrigals. Secondly, he was even more interested
in characterization, and he wanted a principal figure who would be
capable of several emotions within a brief space of time—hence his
liking for a mad person who could simulate this in a natural way. This
is an important step forward, and the results of such thinking are
evident in his last operas.

After this Monteverdi had little opportunity for opera for over ten
years, and by that time he was an old man of seventy. He would
probably have never composed a big work again if the new opera
companies of Venice had not been so successful. If the new audience
was not socially very different from that to which Monteverdi was
accustomed at Mantua, it was different in one significant way. It was
not in the least interested in the old academic ideas. It was out for
entertainment, and found it where it had always been found—in the
spectacle. The scenery and the machines became even more important
than before. *Orfeo* could have been produced with about five or six
scenic changes. A score of them was not an uncommon number for a
Venetian opera. As for the music, the audience had never heard of

the discussion about the audibility of the words and the total impression of meaning and emotional sense which had resulted in the recitative style. The Venetian patricians were better acquainted with the arias in the song-books of the last two decades. As for the highly symbolical stories of the earliest operas, they were less interested in mythology and more concerned with human characters, at least in so far as the pastoral drama made them possible.

The two Venetian operas by Monteverdi which have come down to us both show the new style very well. The first of them, *Il ritorno d'Ulisse in patria* (the home-coming of Ulysses), has been held by some scholars to be a spurious work, so different is it from his earlier operas; and admittedly there are difficulties connected with it. The manuscript is now in the National Library in Vienna and no one knows when or how it came to be there. Then the libretto (in St Mark's Library in Venice) and the score are different in many particulars. Finally, it is held to be an inferior work (although this is surely flimsy evidence on which to come to any conclusion). In reply it must be said that stylistically the music is too like Monteverdi to be rejected on this evidence. There are passages in the *stile concitato*—very like the warlike madrigals of Book VIII—a plethora of duets in Monteverdi's style, the *arioso* laments and his general feeling for organization in writing recitative, and, above all, a sense of serious interest in the drama. If the work is not by Monteverdi himself, it is by someone who knew his music extremely well—not a very sensible conclusion to come to.

The story is taken from Homer. Ulysses has spent many years wandering over land and sea. His wife Penelope, though near to despair, is still waiting for him. But now he is near at hand, guided home to Ithaca by the goddess Minerva. Disguised as a beggar, he meets an old shepherd Eumetes, who helps him towards his home, although he does not as yet recognize the king. Ulysses' son, Telemachus, is also brought to meet Eumetes by Minerva, and Ulysses reveals himself. They plan to return to the court and rid Penelope of the unwanted attentions of her suitors, anxious to inherit the king's wealth. Telemachus is sent on ahead and warns Penelope that Ulysses is near. The suitors gather for a final attempt to persuade her to marry one of them, and Penelope suggests that whoever can bend Ulysses' bow shall be her husband. They try, and fail. And then Ulysses himself comes to try—as yet unrecognized by anyone at court. He kills them all with his arrows. Penelope at first cannot believe that the old man is Ulysses, in spite of the assurance of Eumetes and Telemachus; but eventually the opera ends with a triumphant recognition.

This has all the hallmarks of a Monteverdi libretto (and we know from his librettist that he moulded its shape himself in many particulars). There is the great dramatic climax of the trial scene, the situations of Penelope and of Ulysses himself which are so like that which inspired the lament in *Arianna*, a messenger scene when Telemachus arrives at court and a happy duet at the end (there is a similar one in *Poppea*). No less Monteverdian are the complicating features. The audience's need of the grand spectacle suggested to him the use of the old form of intermezzos. So we find a prologue with the allegorical figures of Human Frailty, Fortune and Love, who sing their rather irrelevant introduction in the form of a set of strophic variations (in exactly the same way that Music had introduced *Orfeo*). And at various points in the drama there are interpolations from the gods—especially from Neptune, who gives some excellent opportunities for spectacular sea machines (to make it almost a *favola marittima* like *Le nozze di Tetide*). As usual there had to be some link between gods and humans, and this is provided by Minerva, who carries out the wishes of the gods by turning from time to time into human form. In other words, the opera is again a story with intermezzos, as *Orfeo* had been. From the point of view of the stage manager, this form offers tremendous opportunities, and the score abounds with directions for machines and stage business of one kind and another. From the audience's point of view, it makes the basic progress of the opera a little too diffuse to be really satisfactory. This is a pity since it means that some of Monteverdi's most splendid music will rarely be heard in its proper surroundings.

The outstanding feature of *Orfeo* was the way Monteverdi crowded into it all the musical forms known in 1607, to express a totality of human emotion. *Il ritorno d'Ulisse* does exactly the same thing in terms of 1640. The Venetian ariettas, the older virtuoso *arioso*, the *madrigali guerrieri,* the strophic variation songs, the chamber duets—all are used to express the varied situations. There even seems to be a rather rough but effective idea of characterization in music. The gods, for example, usually maintain their dignity in the *arioso*-recitative of the older operas and intermezzos. Neptune in fact is the natural successor of Charon and Pluto (of *Il ballo delle ingrate*), a deep bass whose words are ponderously painted in conventional musical images, with sudden changes of register. All the gods have highly ornamented and virtuoso parts and are deliberately denied the smoother aria rhythms which would rob them of their superhumanity. Only Minerva is allowed to sing pretty tunes, and only when she appears in human clothes.

Similarly Penelope, unhappy and beset with troubles until the very last scene, is given her character in highly charged emotional recitative. In the first scene we have a re-creation of the glories of Ariadne's lament. Not so dissonant as the model, Penelope's plaint gains its effects by changes in tempo, variations of phrase length and repetitions of phrases. The first climax with its rising sequences of despair and fall of a sixth reminds us so strongly of Monteverdi's earlier music that it is difficult to believe it is by any other composer:

The whole scene is as tightly organized as ever, with the occasional use of memorable fragments to make refrains and give musical power to the recitative. Ulysses is introduced in a similar *scena*, and with recitative scarcely less poignant and powerful. But since in subsequent scenes he is led homewards by Minerva and therefore given hope and a purpose for living, he tends to interrupt the recitative with songs—rarely complete in themselves but expressive of his mood. His music is precisely what Monteverdi had planned in setting the libretto of *Licori*, full of sudden changes to express the detail of the words.

This shows the fine concern for the drama which had been Monteverdi's all his life; and it is confirmed in yet another way. The soliloquy is now less important than the dialogue. Every scene, even if it contains an important aria, manages to weave in an interplay of characters and gives them conversation which is significant dramatically. People talk to people, rather than as in *Orfeo* to the world in general; and this makes it an opera of *ensembles* (as all successful operas are). Not for nothing had Monteverdi written so many duet madrigals. *Il ritorno d'Ulisse* adds to their number. Perhaps the most beautiful of them is the one where Ulysses meets his son Telemachus. It begins in a passionate recitative style and gradually becomes *arioso*, full of the melting suspensions which Monteverdi uses in his most magical chamber duets:

Scarcely less beautiful are the duets between Eumetes and Ulysses in an earlier scene and the final love duet. Both are written mellifluously in triple time, and the first of these is a chaconne of impeccable technique:

Although these pieces and the arias could come straight out of the song-books of the 1630's, they never caused Monteverdi to lose sight of the larger formal patterns required in each scene, and he seeks out every opportunity to give large-scale organization to the music as he had done in *Orfeo*. The scene where the suitors plead with Penelope to marry them is a gift to the composer, who can repeat her refusals and punctuate their individual appeals with a thrice repeated *continuo* madrigal. In the scene where Penelope tests them with Ulysses' bow the relationship of aria and recitative is especially useful. In each case the suitor's aria comes first, to express his confidence. It is only when he tries and fails that the recitative comes—usually broken into short phrases to give the impression of breathlessness. Ulysses, on the other hand, starts in recitative and then breaks into aria as he succeeds; and a *sinfonia da guerra* as he deals with his foes is a particularly effective way of using the *stile concitato*.

Even now we have not mentioned half the beauties or the variety of character to be found in the opera—Penelope's maid, for example, who sings a lovely duet with her lover in the first act, using all the arts of the chamber duet; long-held notes on the voices while the harmonies go on underneath, quasi-recitative, *arioso* and triple-time aria, the last for a particularly seductive refrain; or Iro, the suitors' toady, who has to run away after Ulysses has returned to court and who parodies all the passionate tricks of the virtuoso singer in a scene which deliberately offsets the climax of the opera. Yet, in a way, this very variety is a weakness. The plot never develops steadily as *Orfeo* had done. It is too fussy, and lacks that overwhelming central point which Monteverdi had sought for in his earlier operas. Though it is always dangerous to condemn an opera which one has never seen on the grounds that its drama is not strong enough, it is not too much to say that if *Il ritorno d'Ulisse* is not produced today, the libretto is responsible more than the music.

There is no such excuse for neglecting Monteverdi's last opera, *L'incoronazione di Poppea*. Monteverdi and his librettist, Busenello, chose a historical subject—for the first time in the history of opera. This has some significance for the development of the *genre*; but it was not so important to Monteverdi, to whom Ariadne and Penelope were just as real as Poppaea. What is really significant is that in *L'incoronazione* the intermezzo elements have been considerably reduced. There is the customary allegorical prologue, and allegorical figures appear in the body of the opera. Yet they are interwoven into the progress of the play and never stand completely outside it as the gods do in *Il ritorno d'Ulisse*. Similarly, although there are many possibilities for scenic changes and a splendid production, the drama is developed in longer sections, scene leading into scene in a natural way. There is far less of the fussiness which mars the earlier work, and the dramatic unity is never abandoned merely for the glories of the producer. It is, in fact, a libretto which conforms to most of the criteria which we apply today, and in spite of a large cast there is never over-complication either of plot or character. Variety of human emotion was Monteverdi's principal aim in all his later operas, and in *L'incoronazione* he finds the most dramatic method for exploiting it. In this libretto the same situations affect different characters in different ways. There is a real conflict and hence a real opportunity for the

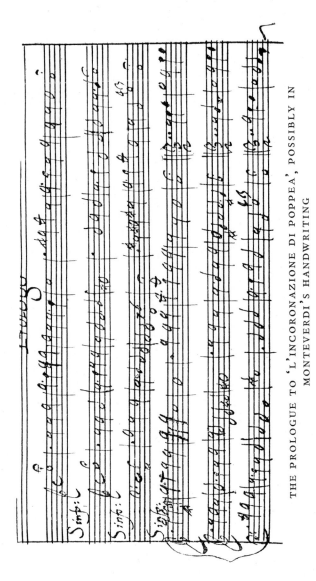

THE PROLOGUE TO 'L'INCORONAZIONE DI POPPEA', POSSIBLY IN
MONTEVERDI'S HANDWRITING

musician to build up characters in a consistent way. The story is taken from Tacitus and moulded into significant scenes, each carefully chosen for its musical possibilities.

Otho, returning from a journey of state, comes home to find soldiers guarding his house. He guesses what has happened. Nero is in love with his wife Poppaea and is visiting her. This is confirmed by the soldiers' conversation and, as the day dawns, by the appearance of Nero with Poppaea herself in the garden. Nero is loath to leave her, but dare not risk a scandal as yet. He declares that he will divorce his wife Octavia and then all will be well. Left alone, Poppaea becomes less the loving woman and shows her vicious ambition. 'Hope and fortune are on my side', she sings. Her nurse, Arnalta, who has joined her in the garden, warns her that these are not the best of allies. We now have a companion scene where Octavia, far from being confident and ambitious, regrets Nero's infidelities. She consults Seneca about her possible courses of action, but his counsel is merely to bear her burden stoically—little comfort indeed either to Octavia or to her page who is standing by her. These two depart, leaving Seneca alone; and suddenly the goddess Pallas Athene is heard (no doubt from some great cloud machine) telling Seneca that he will die that day. He is unmoved by this and looks forward to a better life.

At this point Nero enters (and we notice how Seneca acts as a focal point for several consecutive scenes). Nero tells Seneca that he has resolved to divorce Octavia and marry Poppaea. Seneca warns him that the people will be displeased. Nero becomes petulant and shouts that he cares nothing for the people or for anyone else. He tells Seneca sharply to go away. Poppaea enters (Nero acting as the link between scenes this time) and the two of them sing another love duet. Having put Nero in a good mood, Poppaea then whispers slanders against Seneca, who she fears is an obstacle to her ambitions. Nero orders a soldier to go to Seneca with the sentence of death. Nero departs and Otho enters to make a last attempt at reconciliation with Poppaea (now the linking personality in her turn). She will have nothing to do with him and Otho thinks darkly of murdering her. After his soliloquy Drusilla, one of the ladies of the court and in love with

Otho, comes in and manages to make him say that he loves her. But, 'Drusilla's name is on my lips, Poppaea's is in my heart', he sings. With this the first act ends.

Act II is in three main sections. The first is constructed around Seneca, who receives warning of his impending death from Mercury (the cloud machine again), and then the death sentence comes, borne by Nero's captain. Seneca's friends plead with him not to die, but he bids them prepare his bath, in which he will open his veins and bleed to death. Before the second section there is an intermezzo (in the modern sense)—a flirtation between the page-boy and the young girl; this is clearly to allow for the passage of time. Then we see Nero again with some friends, now celebrating Seneca's death with ribald glee. The third part of the act is taken up with Otho, now almost determined upon the murder of his wife. His doubts are finally overcome by Octavia, who equally wants Poppaea out of the way. They plot to dress up Otho as a woman: in this disguise he is to gain entrance to Poppaea's room. They leave, and we next see Drusilla, happily confident in the love of Otho. He enters to borrow her clothes, which she gives him quite willingly. Now the moment of murder approaches. The scene is again Poppaea's garden, where she falls asleep while her nurse sings a lullaby. Then the god of love enters and sings yet another lullaby. The disguised Otho comes in and is just about to strike when the god (perhaps with an intricate movement of the cloud machine) stops him. Poppaea wakes up, and seeing the prospective murderer running away thinks it was Drusilla.

The final act begins with an aria by Drusilla. She is interrupted by Poppaea's nurse, who comes in with guards and identifies her as the attacker. Drusilla protests her innocence but Nero enters and threatens her with tortures if she does not tell the plot. She confesses to the crime to save her beloved Otho. Nero is ordering an exceptionally cruel death for her as Otho himself arrives, to confess his own guilt and Octavia's. Nero, realizing that it is Octavia who is ultimately to blame, banishes Otho, who departs with Drusilla. Nero announces his divorce and the banishment of Octavia. The final scene is the brilliant coronation of the new empress, Poppaea.

This detailed synopsis of the plot reveals some of the reasons why it is a masterpiece. The excellence of the libretto lies in the way it avoids unnecessary explanations and makes the reasons of the heart compelling. Nero, for example, acts in a predictable way in every situation and is seen in enough differing situations to appear as a complete man. He is amorous but sad on leaving Poppaea, petulant when Seneca disagrees with him, cruel with Drusilla, revoltingly gay with his friends and amorous and content at the end of the opera. Equally, Poppaea is flirtatious, ambitious and hard, triumphant and sensuously happy in turn. Monteverdi's power in expressing these differing emotions is beyond all praise. At the places where we expect him to be good he is magnificent—as in the love duets which derive from the madrigal books and yet outdo them in sensuousness. And it is the music which gives great variety to the love-making. The opening duet between Nero and Poppaea is full of longing, dissonances and minor harmonies predominating, and fragments of aria always being interrupted by recitative. The two voices never sing together, and their motif 'addio' is repeated time after time in harmonies which do not resolve, as they cannot break away from one another. Their final duet, on the contrary, is a smooth chaconne, the dissonances always resolving promptly and the melody continuous even when shared between the voices. The harmony has the usual richness of Monteverdi's duets, and as the bass repeats itself so their happy love seems endless.

Neither of these is like the duet between Nero and Lucan when, Seneca dead, the bachelor party thinks lustfully of Poppaea's charms. Again Monteverdi writes a triple-time chaconne, but this time while Lucan sings a *bel canto* melody, Nero can do no more than gasp, 'Ah what a destiny', in single notes or short phrases:

The love duet between the page and the girl which comes just before this in Act II is also completely different. This is light-hearted flirtation, the boy singing a song which might have come out of the *Scherzi musicali*, the girl taking it more seriously and more confidently in a smooth triple-time aria before they finally join rapturously together.

As always, there are laments, and very fine ones. Of the several set pieces the one sung by Octavia, leaving Rome for ever, inevitably reminds us of *Arianna*. Compounded of short pregnant phrases, it makes the same use of dissonance and has the same power of changing its mood rapidly, by changing from declamation to *arioso*. Drusilla's agony when falsely accused is shorter and part of a dialogue but is not less taut and gripping. Otho's opening scene is equally expressive. He starts in happy *arioso* as he asks Poppaea to open the door of the balcony, even breaking into a felicitous aria. Then he sees the soldiers. The recitative at once becomes agonized, broken and dissonant, and at its climax becomes obsessed with a tiny motif as the librettist piles up the appealing phrases: 'I am that Otho who followed you, who longed for you, who served you—that Otho who adored you.' These are offshoots of Monteverdi's earlier music. There are other moments which are quite unexpected. The use of the *stile concitato* is new, for it not only occurs to express the usual external images of war (as when the soldiers are talking in Act I) but also to conjure up the emotions of wrath and cruelty. Nero's anger when Seneca refuses to fall in with his wishes provokes an outburst which shows very clearly the immaturity of a monarch who has always had his own way:

A similarly pungent passage comes when Drusilla is interrogated in the last act.

The trio in Act II is also unusual for Venetian opera. Sung by Seneca's friends imploring him not to commit suicide, it is a most moving chromatic piece which culminates in a series of agonized cries: 'Non morir, non morir, Seneca, no!' The final surprise, perhaps, is the memorability of the melody. Not that Monteverdi had ever been untuneful, but in this opera he surrenders a number of times to the charms of the Venetian song-books. Poppaea's aria after Nero has gone in Act I, Drusilla's song (a perfect *da capo* aria) as she awaits Otho, and the two lullabies in Act III are extremely attractive in themselves. These and the others are mainly in triple time, and because of their clear rhythm and lucid diatonic melody (although Monteverdi has a mannerism of juggling with alternate major and minor thirds), they stick effortlessly in the mind.

'Ariadne moved the audience because she was a woman, and

equally Orpheus because he was a man and not a wind.' This philosophy reaches its most practical realization in *L'incoronazione di Poppea*. Like Mozart and Verdi, Monteverdi saw that it was necessary to have a sufficiently large and contrasting cross-section of humanity with which to create the world of opera, and that all the resources of music would be needed to bring these characters to life. The only larger criticism which can be brought against the opera is that the strange morality of ancient Rome is too vividly drawn. The characters and situations are so alive that to end with the glorification of an evil couple at first sight seems rather revolting. And yet it is satisfying. As Wagner said of the ending of *Götterdämmerung*, when it was pointed out to him that with the gold returned to the Rhine-maidens there was no reason why the gods should perish, the emotional logic of art demands the destruction of Valhalla. Monteverdi also knew this kind of logic. *L'incoronazione di Poppea* is a great opera.

CHAPTER VII

THE CHURCH MUSIC

THE obsession of the last hundred and fifty years with the music of Palestrina and his followers has almost completely obscured the complexity of church music in the later sixteenth century. Counter-Reformation church music has the same complications as the Counter-Reformation itself. The Roman Church could have within its ranks evangelists with such differing methods as the Oratorians of St Philip Neri and the Jesuits. Its church musicians contain equally diverse figures. Palestrina, Victoria, the Gabrielis, Lassus and the host of cathedral musicians seem at times to have little in common with one another. To try to see them as part of a single movement is to despair of finding a general pattern. If there is a common denominator to be found, it is one of principle rather than of style or technique. The principle is a familiar one—that the words must fertilize the music and not act merely as its excuse. This was the demand of the Council of Trent no less than of the humanists who helped opera to come into being. But principle is one thing; its application is another. Just as the interpretations of the Greek theorists gave rise to a host of differing musical styles, so in church music we can find several interpretations of the basic idea, all of them valid and defensible.

There was, first of all, the demand that the words should be audible. The church had its own monody ready made in plainsong. Palestrina and one of his colleagues, Zoilo, were set to revise the missal and breviary. Then as now, plainsong was not always sung unaccompanied. The support of the organ was quite often needed, and this gave rise to yet another sort of music in which the words were heard clearly —the harmonized chanting known as *falso bordone*. Here the composer provided some simple chords and left the words to be chanted in speech rhythm, breaking into polyphony only at the end of each section of the text. This, at least, was the theory. In practice, singers found it far too elementary to satisfy their desires and they often added ornaments to the chant in an ornate, not to say extravagant, manner.[1] *Falso bordone* was the favoured medium in setting the psalms for vespers. Its popularity probably rested on simplicity of performance, and scores of books were published in the later years of the century.

Audibility was a prime consideration in the other popular outlet for composition, the *missa brevis*. Here the composer admittedly imposed a musical rhythm on the words, but in the *Gloria* and *Credo* at least he followed the injunction 'to every syllable a note' (the phrase is Archbishop Cranmer's, and it is interesting to see similar ideas developing in the music of the liturgies of the Roman and Anglican faiths). Elsewhere in the Mass the composer was allowed imitative counterpoint and melismatic melody. Even so, the *missa brevis* shows a strong tendency towards homophonic writing and therefore an increased interest in harmonic devices. This is not to say that the tradition of conventional polyphony disappeared, merely that it was not alone. Yet it too shows some effect of counter-reform in the widening gap between secular and religious music. Gone were the parody Masses on secular songs. Thematic material was now taken from plainsong or polyphonic motets. Palestrina's conscious attempts to produce consonant harmony from smoothly flowing melodic lines contrast powerfully with the growing dissonance and rugged melody of the madrigal. The asceticism of the Jesuits has its counterpart in this music.

But the asceticism of the Jesuits was achieved through the sensuous *Spiritual exercises* of St Ignatius Loyola. Nor were they averse to using the sensuousness of art to impress and overwhelm the common people. This too has its counterpart in the splendid church music written for the ducal chapels of northern Italy. These had the resources to give church music a glamour which, if it reflected the glory of the prince or doge, was not unsuitable for praising an all-powerful God. *Castrati*, a big choir and a large group of instrumentalists could stimulate the church composer's imagination as well as that of an opera composer or madrigalist. In St Mark's in Venice and St Barbara in Mantua this was exploited to the full.

[1] The Sistine Chapel's singing of Allegri's *Miserere* in Holy Week is a good example of how it was done.

The Church Music

Wert's church music, for example, shows that he made virtually no distinction between secular and religious music. When in his early life he was composing in a predominantly Netherlandish style, his church music was contrapuntal in the traditional way. But there is none of the asceticism of Palestrina about it. It is full of rhythmic life, with jaunty syncopations and cross-rhythms, and its harmony has that lively roughness which disappears from contrapuntal music only when the Roman school has become the chosen model. When Wert's madrigal style changes about 1580, his church music changes with it. The expression of the words becomes all important, and dissonance and chromaticism are as essential a part of his church music as of his madrigals, e.g. in the motet, *Vox in Rama*:

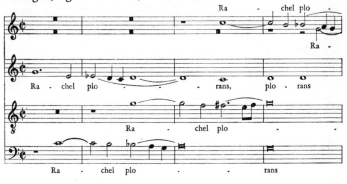

The large awkward leaps which we have seen in such madrigals as *Solo e pensoso* appear in the motets too, and for the same purpose. For joyful moments Wert's natural virility of rhythm turns almost to dance music, as rolling sequential phrases produce clear-cut strong accents, e.g. in *Amen, amen*:

In this later music of Wert and in the motets of the younger men, Pallavicino and Gastoldi, the Venetian style begins to predominate. This is based on the *cori spezzati*—choirs widely separated in the church and alternating with one another throughout a motet or

Mass. In the first place this means of expression, based as it was on ancient Jewish practice and simple in its homophonic declamation of the words (necessary to ensure *ensemble* at all), might well have been ordered by the reformers of Trent. By the 1580's, however, it had become rather debased. The Venetian love of orchestral colour saw that the emphasis was placed less on the words than on the grandeur of effect. Some of the 'choirs' now became groups of instruments with soloists placed among them. From these special effects were produced. Echo music was one favourite, even though it almost blasphemously turned 'clamor' to 'amor' and 'clamat' to 'amat'. Dialogue motets dramatizing the speeches of saints and apostles were also popular. As for the orchestra, it took its part in sumptuous canzonas and sonatas played during the Mass or vespers. There was, then, a tremendously varied choice before the composer of church music. In practice his style was conditioned as always by the resources to hand. At Cremona, for example, Ingegneri hardly needed to concern himself with the grand manner. He had instrumentalists for some of the greater festivals, but of necessity his music grew out of small resources. His music naturally follows the contrapuntal school, rather less austere than Palestrina's and more like the earlier church music of Wert. He is not averse to an occasional chromaticism, but expressiveness is not his main consideration.

Monteverdi's *Sacrae cantiunculae*, the work of a boy of fifteen, are an offshoot of such conservatism. They are *tricinia*, that is, motets for three voices; and this, coupled with the fact that the texts in question are for the most part unliturgical, suggests that they were probably meant for private devotions rather than for public performance. For domestic singing they are ideal. The melodic lines are always interesting—a thing not to be taken for granted at a time when composers were becoming more concerned with the total effect of vocal colour. Nor are they ever really difficult, for they remain largely diatonic and are constructed from the more familiar motifs and decorative figures. Monteverdi at this stage in his career was rather inconsistent in the way that he decorated unimportant words with melismas while often ignoring expressive ones; but this is something we might expect of a boy, for the manipulation of words is often no little embarrassment to a beginner whose main concern is making the counterpoint fit together. As for the counterpoint itself, it is very efficient indeed, with a pure consonant harmony and the skilfully overlapping phrases which maintain the contrapuntal flow. The *Sacrae cantiunculae* are not works of genius. It is enough that they are indistinguishable from countless other *tricinia* of the epoch.

At Mantua the choice became a real one. Everything was known there. We know from the descriptions of Duke Vincenzo's coronation that Wert commanded resources of Venetian sumptuousness. From the publications of Pallavicino and Gastoldi we learn that *falso bordone*, separated choirs and large contrapuntal music were used in St Barbara. Whether Monteverdi added to these works is not known. It seems probable that until Gastoldi left for Milan in 1609 his duties led him only to compose chamber music and opera. By the time that he did come to compose church music, the choice had widened even further, for the *basso continuo* altered church music just as much as it had changed the madrigal. Not that it altered the spirit of church music very much. Viadana's *Concerti* of 1602 are very like the older motets in their melodic writing and their harmonies. They spread the melodic writing among fewer voices and rid themselves of constant imitations. Apart from this they can have sounded very little different from some of the more harmonically conceived *a cappella* motets.

In the larger-scale works much the same thing happened. The Venetian composers now accompanied their soloists with the organ and added groups of soloists to the possible variety of groupings. By the ingenious positioning of these groups the soloists were not drowned by the *ripieno* voices and instruments, and sudden dramatic contrasts were obtained. The only novelty in technique was the increasing sectionalism which soloists engendered. One or two composers took advantage of the contrast between solo passages and *tutti* to insert duets and trios which were more or less complete in themselves and were punctuated by refrains sung by the choir. Finally, there was a continuation of the tradition of secularized church music and the sacred madrigal. Naturally enough the modern equivalent was to introduce monodic techniques into motets—declamatory lines, virtuoso ornaments, rich dissonant harmonies and the rest. This happened rather slowly, largely because the early composers of monody were courtiers and singers, while the church musicians were professional composers; but by about 1608 true sacred monodies were appearing, usually under titles like *Sacri affetti* or *Ghirlanda sacra*, deliberately non-committal about liturgical usage. The texts of these sacred songs come mainly from biblical sources rather than from the liturgy, and mirror the secular song in emotional richness. Like Monteverdi's *Sacrae cantiunculae* they were probably more often heard in the private chambers of the nobility and such members of the higher clergy who had virtuoso singers among their retinue.

The new never replaces the old suddenly, especially in church music, where traditions have always been treasured more than elsewhere. Even so, to find the profusion of styles and techniques that we have in Monteverdi's volume of 1610 is surprising. A Mass in the old polyphonic style, a set of vesper psalms in the grand manner, and a group of monodic *sacri affetti*—these are unusual bedfellows even for this period of change.[1] The explanation is not hard to seek. Trying to find a job outside Mantua he determined to show that he was competent in all fields and was fit for a post either in conservative Rome or scintillating Venice. It is no surprise that the collection was

---

[1] The contents are described as follows on the title-page:

> Missa senis vocibus
> ad ecclesiarum choros
> Ac Vespere pluribus decantandae
> cum nonnullis sacris concentibus
> ad Sacella sive Principum Cubicula accommodata.

That is to say: 'Mass for six voices suitable for church choirs, and vespers to be performed by larger forces (together with some motets) suitable for chapels or the apartments of princes.' In accordance with normal Latin usage *accommodata* goes with both *Missa* and *Vespere*.

never reprinted. Its size and contents suggest that it was a presentation volume, not meant for ordinary practical use.

That the Mass should be written in *a cappella* polyphony is not surprising in a book to please the Roman taste. The form the poly-phony takes is a little overwhelming. Monteverdi takes ten themes from a motet of Gombert (nothing recent or popular, we notice) and then works these out in the strictest possible way. There is none of Palestrina's rapturous delight in choral colour nor Wert's expressive-ness of the words—and no homophonic climax. The work is thick with imitative points. Voices are given rests only to emphasize new imitations, regardless of their breath capacity or proneness to be tired. The only sign of modern taste is in the regularity of the melody, in which the old modal system is replaced by the diatonic scales and sequences, and square rhythms appear quite often. The virility of Netherlandish rhythm and the bite of dissonance are both lacking, and since Monteverdi refuses to make clear even such contrasts as exist between 'Crucifixus' and 'Et resurrexit', the result is a curiously emasculated work. It was a work of great learning for Monteverdi to write, and it sounds like it. Only occasionally, as in the 'Hosanna', does it sound at all natural and alive.

The vespers music reveals Monteverdi's real inclination. This is indeed the work of a North Italian court musician. The big orchestra, the solo singers and the choir are all there, and the music reflects the worldly grandeur of prince and doge.[1] And whereas no one could find anything Monteverdian in the 'Gombert Mass', the vespers bear the imprint of his style, above all in the taste for compromise—the interest in putting old means to new uses. Separated choirs, *falso bordone*, the traditional Venetian canzona are the materials. Every one of them is given a new twist. The opening versicle and response, *Domine ad*

[1] The word 'big' is relative. If, as is probable, the vesper psalms were his test pieces for St Mark's, Venice, it is of interest to note that the account books show that he had an orchestra of six resident players and twenty specially hired for the occasion, and a choir of about twenty-five. Two extra organs had to be brought from St Mark's Seminary.

adiuvandum, for example, is really written in *falso bordone.* The choir chants on a single chord except at the very end. This is conventional enough. If the instruments had doubled them in some way it would have been completely conventional. But Monteverdi has given them music of their own to play—an adaptation of the toccata which had opened *Orfeo.* As an instrumental piece it is sonorous; with a choir adding sonority but not any thematic material to distract the ear from it, its splendour is increased.

The five psalm settings use an equally traditional technique, that of the *cantus firmus.* Each is founded on a psalm-tone, which is repeated several times, often altered very freely in rhythm. Super-imposed on this pattern is one of the common techniques of the early seventeenth century. In the first one, *Dixit Dominus,* the pre-dominant method is to mingle passages in *falso bordone* with duets and trios for solo voices. The organ bass over which these solos develop is the *cantus firmus,* giving the effect of strophic variation in the manner of the *continuo* madrigal. Each *falso bordone* section flowers into the traditional polyphony, which is expanded by instrumental repetition. These sections at first sight seem more revolutionary than they really are. One dance-like passage is in fact almost identical with Wert's motet *Amen, amen* quoted above (page 134); another is a common contrapuntal tag; yet another, highly ornamented, merely writes down what had been improvised by singers for many years, as a glance at the treatises on ornaments shows us. Even the solo sections are restrained—Viadana-like rather than secular in origin.

The first page of *Laudate pueri* looks quite conservative. It develops in the manner of a large contrapuntal piece by Andrea Gabrieli, announcing its plainsong theme with a jaunty rhythm and working it to a climax in polyphony. Only then does Monte-verdi start with the *concertato* technique which reminds us of the fifth book of madrigals. A series of trios ensues, one part singing the plainsong, the others decorating extravagantly. This is really secular in style; and after some double-choir interjections in triple time there is a voluptuous duet which is very like parts of *Ahi come a un vago sol:*

N.B. The right hand of the organ doubles the voices.

Laetatus sum uses a similar technique, except that here Monteverdi gives an added importance to the organ bass, which gives out a theme in crotchets and acts as an anchor in much the same way that the plainsong had done in *Dixit Dominus*. The actual chant is split up among the voices as the piece proceeds. Again Monteverdi draws clear contrasts, this time between the quasi-contrapuntal trios and quartets and sections in which *falso bordone* is left either as a simple chant or as the basis for voluptuous improvisation.

The other two psalms are more conventional. *Nisi Dominus* is a big double-choir setting in which the *cantus firmus* appears in long notes in the tenor part of each choir. Although the use of *cori spezzati* hardly ever fails to fascinate, the piece is constructed in too long sections, with a great deal of repetition, and lacks the cut and thrust of Gabrielian dialogue. The sonorities of the final climax are magnificent, but it is not consistently interesting. *Lauda Jerusalem*, on the other hand, is very exciting throughout. Though it uses contrasting groups from time to time, it is really a piece in the manner of Wert. The smooth unexciting rhythms of Palestrina are quite foreign to it, and the syncopations are given added force by a regularly changing harmony.

To match the grandeur of these psalms in the hymn *Ave maris stella* presented Monteverdi with a new problem. Hymns were normally sung in plainsong in Venice, and the only models to hand were the rather old-fashioned settings by Wert. Monteverdi's setting of the first verse is rather like these, with its eight independent lines following their own rhythms to give a complicated texture in which the rhythmicized plainsong in the *cantus* part is sometimes a little obscured. Then he has a brilliant new idea. He turns the plainsong, one of the most beautiful of hymn melodies, into a song in triple time, engagingly serene in its balanced, *hemiolia* accentuation. One choir sings a simple harmonization of it; the other repeats it; and then three soloists (the bass as usual being left out) sing in their turn, accompanied by the organ. In between these middle verses a *ritornello* in triple time is given to the instruments to provide a rest from the tune. The opening contrapuntal setting rounds off the piece in the final verse.

All this music is liturgical. The *Sonata sopra Sancta Maria* is only loosely so. The words 'Sancta Maria, ora pro nobis' come from the litany of the Blessed Virgin, but the idea of an orchestral piece around them is purely north Italian. Monteverdi borrowed it from a Ferrarese composer called Crotti. A fragment of plainsong is sung by a soloist eleven times. Around it the instruments play a *canzona francese* complete with the stereotyped rhythm and *da capo* form which are its hallmarks. These are the bare bones of the piece; but such a bald description does no justice to the tremendous invention that Monteverdi brings to it. Whereas Crotti's piece had been a small-scale chamber *canzona*, Monteverdi turns it into a splendid sonata in the Venetian manner—in fact, one of the largest orchestral pieces of its time. We have a swinging tune which turns into a triple-time variation in the way in which a pavane becomes a galliard, a series of *ensembles* in which each separate element of the orchestra is exploited to the full, virtuoso dotted rhythms and sequential phrases, and the initial *canzona* tune forming a climax by being played simultaneously with the plainsong *cantus firmus* at the end. Here is a magnificence which Crotti never knew.

Magnificence and splendour are recurring words in any account of this vespers music. They represent something quite new in Monteverdi's work. In the madrigals it is an intimate power which he commands, and grandeur is an extension of his range. The natural continuation of his earlier style is to be found in the *sacri affetti* (interspersed among the psalms) and the Magnificats which complete this volume of church music. The four motets for soloists were the first chamber music by Monteverdi in the style of the 'new music' to be published, and they show that the seventh book of madrigals of almost ten years later was given lengthy preparation.

The one solo motet, *Nigra sum*, is a setting of some voluptuous verses from the *Song of Songs*:[1] 'I am black, but comely, O ye daughters of Jerusalem. Therefore the king hath loved me and hath brought me in to his chambers and hath said to me: "Rise up, my love, and com eaway."' The relationship of the text to the words of Monteverdi's secular music needs no explanation. He puts on his finest *seconda prattica* manner and writes a monody which might well come from an opera. His capacity for inventing the memorable phrase, for fitting the music to the detail of the words, is displayed at its best. This can hardly be shown more completely than in the way Monteverdi isolates the king's words, 'Rise up, my love', with a preliminary rest, and then writes rapturously persuasive music for the constant repetition of the word 'surge', the shortening phrases melting into the continuous climactic phrase:

[1] A conflation of i. 4–5 and ii. 10.

As in the recitatives of *Orfeo*, the musical shape is always of primary importance. The motif set to the words 'Nigra sum' inevitably comes again, and the final section of the motet is repeated, even though there is no reason for it in the words.

The duet, *Pulchra es*, is another setting of verses from the *Song of Songs*. It is Monteverdi's first chamber duet and it needs little description here simply because it shows complete mastery of all the technical devices of the duets in the later madrigal books. The second voice amplifies the phrases, gives harmonic fullness and expands the scale of the music in just the same way. There is the same ability to organize the ornaments of the melody into satisfying patterns, and to change the mood abruptly with an alteration of harmony or a move from *arioso* to declamation. This is fine music and is capped only by a yet finer motet, *Duo Seraphim*. If it were not for its tenor clefs, this would look like a piece for the Ferrara ladies who so bored the ambassador Urbini. All the resources of ornamentation are deployed—sobbing trills, dotted notes and scale-wise melismas—and given to all the three voices they produce a marvellously rich effect. We are meant to admire the virtuosity, and we do. But true greatness is given to the piece by other things: the way the third voice, brought in to express the mystery of the Three (a triad) in One (a unison), is then retained for the repetition of the word 'Sanctus', making it still richer and more flowing; and the opening of the motet itself with its wonderful series of suspensions:

With *Audi, coelum* we come to the almost inevitable echo piece. But this does not remind us of the Venetian choral dialogues. It is a descendant of a piece by Peri for a Florentine intermezzo. The descending sixth in the melody, the passionate reiteration of the word 'Maria'

SELVA
MORALE E SPIRITVALE

DI CLAVDIO MONTEVERDE

Maeſtro Di Capella della Sereniſſima
Republica Di Venetia

DEDICATA

ALLA SACRA CESAREA MAESTA DELL' IMPERATRICE

ELEONORA
GONZAGA

Con Licenza de Superiori & Priuilegio.

SOPRANO  Primo

IN VENETIA MDCXXXX

Appreſſo Bartolomeo Magni

---

each time decorated anew and the careful declamation are the results of *seconda prattica* thinking. Nor are the echoes ever applied mechanically, for they are used to expand the phrases and add emphasis. Even when the full choral group is brought in at the end to express the words 'let us all therefore follow her', the solo and its echo maintain the sensuous mood as they sing the words 'miseris solamen' (the last word producing the echo 'amen', to lead music and words towards the ending).

Monteverdi provides two Magnificats, one for the large group of instrumentalists and voices needed for the psalm settings, the other simply for voices and organ. Both use the same techniques, and if we discuss the larger one it is because it is easier to see in this the union of the grand manner and the sacred monody. The Magnificat was traditionally a sectional work, with duets and trios interspersed between sections for the *tutti* of five or six voices. No doubt these contrasts were accentuated further when instruments took part. Where Monteverdi is original is in conceiving the work in such a way that instruments, solo and *ripieno* voices are each given something to do which only they can do well. He turns the Magnificat into twelve sections (ten verses and the doxology), and each of them is treated in a different way. The only common feature to them all is the plainsong *cantus firmus* which appears in long notes throughout. A choral setting of the first one gives way to a soprano, who sings the plainsong while the organ decorates. Two tenors weave their dotted notes and roulades round the alto in the next one, and then as a tenor sings out the plainsong, duets of instruments (flutes followed by trombones for the words 'the lowliness of his handmaiden', and recorders for the angelic 'call me blessed') enrich the texture. Violins with ornamental figuration are included in the next section. The fifth section returns to the voices alone, who sing a choral dialogue with contrasting upper and lower groups in the manner of a motet by Giovanni Gabrieli, *Beata es Virgo*.

After this first climax the humanity of the Virgin's song increasingly infects the music. The seventh section is in fact an operatic *scena*. The tenor sings of the abasement of the mighty; and cornetts and violins each in pairs, echo one another with the same magic that Orpheus used to bewitch Charon. After more duets and trios the two tenors sing another echo song, to the glory of the Father, Son and Holy Ghost. Their fine disregard for accurate declamation and their splendidly virtuoso phrases make this one of the most passionate moments in a passionate work:

Then, and only then, are the instruments allowed to double the voices to give a noble conclusion to the work.

Passion and magnificence—these two are inseparable words in

describing the volume, and a detailed analysis of it is necessary in any study of Monteverdi's music, since it shows the determined path for his later religious work. In Venice he developed passion in more *sacri affetti* and magnificence in the motets for festival days, not to mention the *a cappella* polyphony for ordinary use in St Mark's. The publishers sought the first of these, and sacred songs and duets by Monteverdi appeared in most of the anthologies of the time. He maintains in them a complete stylistic unity with his secular chamber music, never becoming deliberately conservative in any way. The four motets published in Simonetti's *Ghirlanda sacra* in 1625 are typical. Two of them, *Ecce sacrum paratum* and *Currite, populi*, are Venetian arias, both having extended triple-time passages interrupted by recitatives. The triple-time sections are completely diatonic, and the 'alleluia' refrain of *Currite, populi* is a lively tune which Berti or Grandi would have been pleased to write for their song-books:

This was an especially popular style, and Monteverdi wrote several of these lighter works, of which two solo motets, *Exulta, figlia*, and *Venite, videte*, are very attractive.[1]

[1] Not in the Collected Edition; reprinted in W. Osthoff, *12 composizioni vocali . . . (inedite)*, Milan, 1958.

The other two motets from the Simonetti *Ghirlanda sacra, O quam pulchra es* and *Salve Regina*, are among the most beautiful of solo madrigals. Both are *arioso* contemplations, and rapturous ones, of womanhood, settings of texts which were especially popular in Venice, where the Blessed Virgin was specially venerated. *O quam pulchra es* begins with Monteverdi's favourite downward sixth in the melody and then lavishes the extravagances of trill and melisma to express the beauty of the beloved. As usual, Monteverdi seizes on the chance to give his melody shape. The short phrases, 'Amica mea, colomba mea, formosa mea', suggest the repetition of a motif; and each time the opening words, 'O how beautiful you are', come round the *gorgia* returns. The climax comes as the lover 'languishes of love' with a chromatic bass pushing the belated melody down to form voluptuous dissonances.

Salve Regina is more serene, although it too has a touch of chromatic desire as the singer sends up 'our sighs, mourning and weeping' in his prayer to the Virgin. It is a piece of long phrases (not so usual for Monteverdi) organized at the beginning by a rhythm suggested by the repetition of the word 'salve' and given variety by sudden bursts of rhythmic energy—'ad te clamamus' or 'eja ergo, o advocata nostra'. Dissonance is reserved for the climax and the inevitable downward sixth comes in the very last phrase.

These motets are fine because they draw out the inner meaning of the words. But Monteverdi is not averse to painting the outer meaning any more than he was in the Tasso settings of his madrigal books. The motet, *Ab aeterno ordinata sum*, for bass, with its description of the creation of the world, is reminiscent of the recitatives of Charon and Pluto in its leaps to the depths for words such as 'abissos' and runs for 'aquis'. *Laudate Dominum*, published in the *Selva morale* of 1640, follows up the mood of *Zefiro torna* and *Armato il cor*. Some details are painted in the *stile concitato* (suggested by the warlike instruments mentioned in the psalm) and both the chaconne bass and the melody which develops over it—with *hemiolias*, held notes and descriptive melismas—are very like the secular duets. Even the sudden change from triple time to the quasi-recitative (not really justifiable in the psalm setting) brings *Zefiro torna* to our mind.

These works, then, are recognizably Monteverdian. This certainly cannot be said of the *prima prattica* Masses and psalms which we find in Vincenti's collected editions of Monteverdi's church music. Here he limits dissonance to suspensions and passing notes on the weak beats, and writes smooth melodic lines in the overlapping phrases which necessarily preclude any dynamic contrasts. These works are consciously archaic; but they are not self-consciously learned as the 'Gombert Mass' had been. Monteverdi composes in an idiom familiar to his age. Completely tonal melody, rhythms which are moulded by the bar-line, the harmonic language of the *missa brevis* rather than the exaggerated imitative counterpoint of 1610—all these give him plenty of scope for writing expressive music. The *Crucifixus* of the Mass published in 1650 uses suspensions most beautifully to express the words 'Passus et sepultus est', and there is genuine excitement in the triple-time 'Et resurrexit' and the sequential phrases of the 'Hosanna'.

The same is true of the psalms for double choir, which bear little relationship to the idiom of the Gabrielis. The dialogue interplay of the older Venetians is there, but the rhythms are rather square and the harmony is deliberately more consonant, more Roman than Venetian. The interest in sheer sonority is restricted to the effects which can be obtained from two equally balanced choirs which never use the extremes of the voice. Even so, the idiom is consistent and has a dignity of its own, though it remains impersonal. The true successors of the grand Venetian motets are to be found in the works written in the *stile concertato*. The grandeur, like Venice's own, becomes slightly diminished as the century proceeds. The huge variety of the Gabrielian orchestra is reduced in Monteverdi's work to a body of strings, sometimes with brass instruments, brought in to support the voices. At the same time he develops the idiomatic use of this orchestra in the way we have seen in the Magnificat of 1610. The instruments rarely double the voices, and then only at climaxes. They add material which is not really suitable for the voices, or else use the vocal material separately to contrast with the choral colour.

It is often said of these works that they are truly secular, and it is certainly true that they often use the same kind of material as Monteverdi's later *continuo* madrigals. One setting of the psalm, *Beatus vir*, for example, uses *Chiome d'oro* from the seventh book of madrigals as its basic material. The warlike phrases of the eighth book appear a number of times in the church music—in the *Nisi Dominus* for six voices and, delightfully, to express the words 'He hath shown strength with his arm' in a Magnificat setting, to exactly the same figure that appears in the *Sinfonia da guerra* when Ulysses has equally shown the strength of his arm. Yet these works do not have the same inner spirit of Monteverdi's madrigals and they do not have the same power of expression. The reason is not, as has been suggested, a spiritual so much as a musical one. With the liturgical music which was needed for St Mark's there was no question of specially choosing or reorganizing the words as in the madrigals. Many of the texts to be set were long, and as yet the new *basso continuo* motet had not evolved a form suited to making such settings continuously interesting. Some of the younger men were working on the right lines. Grandi divided his psalms into sections which were more or less complete in themselves; Tarquinio Merula was experimenting with sections bound together with *ostinato* figures. Monteverdi preferred rather conservatively to stick to the long duet and trio sections which Viadana had evolved. The result is that many of these works, while containing fertile ideas, do not hang together.

But where Monteverdi sees a real opportunity for large-scale organization, he writes church music that is both expressive of the words and worthily splendid in the Venetian tradition. Perhaps the most splendid of all his church music is to be found in the *Gloria* with trombones and strings which he composed in 1631 for the Mass in thanksgiving for the relief from the plague. The liturgical text suited him, for it was not unmanageably long and it had contrasting ideas to offset its general mood of rejoicing. The tenor intones with a lively rhythm, and then through a series of duets Monteverdi works up a motif into a tremendous climax:

[*continued on page* 152

'Peace on earth' suggests a homophonic passage for the full choir, using the lower register of all the voices, just as in the peaceful section of *Hor che 'l ciel e la terra*. Then there is a series of duets, two-bar phrases for tenors or sopranos being answered or echoed by a pair of violins. The words 'Gloria tua' suggest the opening motif again, and it is given to each of the voices in turn; but, very skilfully, it is not worked up to the massive climax of the first section and is deliberately broken off for more duet work. 'Qui tollis' is set in duet and trio texture held together with a *ritornello*. When Monteverdi comes to

F

'In gloria Dei Patris' he naturally brings back the beginning, and this time there is no interruption. The opening climax comes back with the increased force of complete thematic recapitulation after a broken development.

This form comes naturally out of the words. Elsewhere Monteverdi has to impose it on them. In the *Beatus vir*, in which he parodies *Chiome d'oro*, the *ostinato* bass of the madrigal comes to his aid; but even then he makes his opening vocal motif return from time to time to make a rondo, and a rondo which is the clearer because the memorable violin figure of the *Chiome d'oro ritornello* usually comes back with it.

The variations on the bass take the form of painting the image of the verse. 'Gloria' provides a sequential, lively, melismatic figure; 'irascetur' a semiquaver motif, and so on. Even so, the piece is slightly too long, not because a short song is difficult to develop into a long psalm (sixteenth-century composers had developed them into complete Mass settings), but because the interplay between the various pairs of voices often leads Monteverdi into short phrases which never grow into something longer and more significant.

He solved the problem in the third setting of *Laudate Dominum* which he included in the *Selva morale*. Here he wrote a duet for sopranos with a choir joining in from time to time to give the appearance of a rondo. In the duet section, the phrases have to develop—and very attractive they are:

The great climax comes when the sopranos' phrases are given to the full choir and extended with repetitions; thereafter Monteverdi is content to leave the doxology to the sopranos alone. Another solution was in his setting of *Confitebor tibi* in the French style. The piece resembles *Dolcissimo uscignolo* from the eighth book of madrigals, both in its rhythms (square two-bar phrases and a lack of dotted notes) and in the way the soprano soloist sings each section and then is greeted with a full harmonization of it by the choir. With its consonant harmony and easy-flowing melody it has the same charm as the secular piece. And then, as the word 'Gloria' comes, Monteverdi lets out an impassioned and triumphant cry from the soprano:

This, if proof is still needed, must convince us of the sincere and deep conviction which made Monteverdi turn to the priesthood at the end of his life.

CHAPTER VIII

REPUTATION AND INFLUENCE

'THE greatest fame which a man may have on earth.' With these words Follino coaxed Monteverdi back to Mantua to compose *Arianna*. Was the promise fulfilled? The question is of some impor-tance to a biographer, and the search for an answer has a twofold value. The reputation that a composer had in his lifetime reveals the manner of man which he appeared to be to his contemporaries. The reputation that his name has acquired in the years since his death throws light on our attitude towards him. To study both these things can therefore help us to avoid the more obvious errors of appraisal and prevent our reading into his life and work merely what we would like to find there. At the same time, it must be admitted that the evidence which we possess is insufficient to give us anything like a complete picture of the growth of Monteverdi's fame. Nor can it tell us how deeply his art affected other composers, for many things which today seem exclusively Monteverdian were in fact the common language of his day. We can, however, deduce certain attitudes, certain pre-ferences for and antipathies to his music which are revealing and significant.

Monteverdi came into prominence comparatively slowly. This is quite clear from the lack of reprints of his early music. The popular anthologies to which composers were invited to contribute by editors and publishers contain little of his music in his early years. While he was living at Cremona this was understandable enough. For his first years at Mantua it is significant. Living among Wert, Pallavicino and Gastoldi he must have had every opportunity to be brought in touch with the Venetian publishers. Apparently this was of no avail. Fewer than half a dozen pieces of his music appeared in his first seven or eight years there. The only reason for this lack of quick success can be that he was not considered a composer of light-weight or occasional music. He was essentially a serious composer who made few concessions to his audience. This is not contradicted by his sudden leap into fame after the production of *Orfeo*. His music then seemed to take on a new lease of life. A large number of editions of all his madrigal books, a large number of contributions to the anthologies display his widening audience—a large number, that is, until we look at the work of somebody like Marenzio, whose work appeared in anthology after anthology for over twenty years, and whose madrigal books rarely went through fewer than five or six reprints.

This sudden success appears to be due to the enthusiasm of connoisseurs. It lasted about six or seven years, during which the fourth and fifth books of madrigals found a special favour. Adriano Banchieri at this time could write in his *Conclusioni del suono dell' organo*; [1]

I must not omit the name of the most sweet composer of music in the modern style, Claudio Monteverdi, head of music to the Most Illustrious Sig. D. Vicenzo Gonzaga, Duke of Mantua (universally well known to the professional musician is his work), since his expression of the emotions, full of art, is truly worthy of complete commendation.

How rapidly things had changed. A few years earlier the same Bolognese writer and composer had acknowledged the receipt of Artusi's vicious attack on Monteverdi in these terms:

I have examined it all, and I say that the book is worthy of eternal praise, for rebutting the crudity of certain composers who destroy the good rules of Zarlino, Franchino, Guido and other intelligent writers, among whom, however, are not included the modern followers of the admirable Roman school, and in particular those who write church music, Sig. Gio. Pietro Pallestina [*sic*], and in chamber music Sig. Luca Marenzio. [2]

[1] 1608 ed., pages 57 f.
[2] *Lettere armoniche*, page 94.

This tide of popularity carried Monteverdi to Venice. After his arrival there the reprints of his old madrigal books gradually died away, and the new ones were never accompanied by the same demand from the public. The reason for this was surely that Monteverdi never bothered to follow the fashions. The song-books of his assistants, Grandi and Rovetta, were selling well. Monteverdi, on the other hand, made no concession to public taste until his second book of *Scherzi musicali* was published. By this time a writer could bewail the decline of conventional madrigal singing: 'Nowadays music is not much cultivated any more, for in Rome gentlemen do not indulge in it; nor do they sing with several voices from part-books as they used to in the past.' It is no wonder that Monteverdi's madrigal books, written for his Mantuan virtuosos, gradually faded into the past.

Oddly enough, in spite of this state of affairs in Italy, foreigners began to take to his music. The vogue for madrigals flowered in both Germany and England just late enough to give his works a new lease of life. The Germans had been interested in his work for some years, and the Nuremberg collector Kauffmann and the organist to the King of Denmark Borchgrevinck (a pupil of Giovanni Gabrieli) had both found opportunities to print Monteverdi's madrigals while he was still at Mantua. Then Phalèse, the enterprising publisher living in Antwerp, took them up, and from about 1615 found a market for the third, fourth and fifth books. He had no audience for the sixth book until 1639, and seems to have had no interest in the *continuo* madrigals.

England was slightly behind the times—when choosing Italian madrigals to copy or print it usually relied on the taste of Phalèse. Some Italophiles admittedly knew of Monteverdi's work. The younger Francis Tregian, copying his immense collection of vocal and instrumental music [1] to while away time in the Fleet Prison about

[1] British Museum, Egerton 3665. Several of Monteverdi's madrigals also occur in British Museum, Add. 31440. It has been suggested that this manuscript may be in the hand of the composer's English pupil, Walter Porter (see page 161); see Pamela J. Willetts, 'A neglected source of monody and madrigal', in *Music and Letters*, XLIII (1962), page 332.

1615, put a number of Monteverdi's madrigals into score, including virtually all of Book IV (why he missed out the first number, *Ah dolente partita*, remains a mystery), but he clearly had an abnormal source of supply in Italy. Another lover of things Italian was Henry Peacham, who published his book *The Compleat Gentleman* in 1622 and included a chapter on the art of music. After singling out Marenzio, Vecchi and Croce for high praise, he went on:

There are many other Authors very excellent, as *Boschetto*, and *Claudio de Monte Verde*, equall to any before named; *Giovannioni Ferretti, Stephano Felis, Giulio Rinaldi, Phillipo de Monte, Andrea Gabrieli, Cyprian de Rore, Pallaviceno* [*sic*], *Geminiano*, with others yet living.[1]

Monteverdi is in similar company in another context. One of the earliest biographers of Milton tells us that when Milton was returning home after a journey in Italy he arrived at Venice, whence

. . . when he had spent a Month's time in viewing of that Stately City, and Shipp'd up a Parcel of curious and rare Books which he had pick'd up in his Travels; particularly a Chest or two of choice Musick-books of the best Masters flourishing about that time in *Italy*, namely, *Luca Marenzio, Monte Verde, Horatio Vecchi, Cifa,* the Prince of *Venosa*, and several others,[2]

he returned to France and from there to England.

These were all men who had some special interest in Italian music; but there is no sign that Monteverdi was as popular as Marenzio or Croce with the ordinary madrigal singers. If the two books of *Musica Transalpina* came too early for his music, it is still significant that the manuscript part-books which have come down to us rarely include it either. This perhaps was due quite simply to the fact that the poetry which he set in his madrigals could hardly be translated with the exactness which would make the madrigals coherent and

[1] Op. cit. (1634 edition), page 102.
[2] H. Darbishire, *The Early Lives of Milton* (London, 1932), page 59.

acceptable. Even so, such a theory must remain unproven since we find some of the most literary madrigals of Books III and IV in still stranger surroundings. There are at least four manuscripts of viol music which contain these,[1] among fantasies and dances of such composers as Lupo, Ferrabosco and Wilbye. The anthologists who selected them had good taste and chose the best. What they made of them without the words is a matter for conjecture.

In Italy, meanwhile, it seems clear that it was the professional musicians and composers who were most appreciative of his work. One of the most distinguished composers of monodies, Claudio Saracini, dedicated to Monteverdi the first solo madrigal of his songbook called *Seconde musiche*. Whether or not he was an actual pupil of Monteverdi, the two composers were certainly musical kinsmen. Saracini was one of the composers who developed the passionate *arioso* and the striking harmonic clashes in Monteverdi's manner. Both composers were prone to academic arguments about the importance of monody in 'moving the affections'. More superficially influenced, perhaps, was Alessandro Grandi. He arrived in Venice a little too late to have his style completely founded on the master, and soon acquired an interest in the modern ariettas which were the favourites of the Venetians. In his church music, on the other hand, the change of style after his arrival to be Monteverdi's assistant was too marked for it to be purely a coincidence. From being a writer of conventional, though often beautiful, *concertato* motets he became one of the principal composers of the solo motet, written in the recitative-arioso style which Monteverdi had introduced in the solo music of the Vespers. Refrain techniques and the use of a rhythmic motif distinguished Grandi's work also and lead to the same sort of emotional richness. He even took up the *stile concitato*, and one of his psalm settings is full of the tremolando string passages which he must have learned from *Il combattimento di Tancredi e Clorinda*:

[1] British Museum, Add. 37402–6, Add. 29427; Christ Church, Oxford, 2, 21, 44; and manuscripts in Marsh's Library, Dublin, Z3, 4, 7–12.

Much the same can be said of Cavalli, who certainly borrowed various ideas from Monteverdi. The 'lament' appears in his operas to form a climax as in *Arianna*; and his solo motets have the same complete secularity which we have seen in Monteverdi's music. Even so, the detail of the Monteverdian style is left well behind in his work, which has none of the old-fashioned declamatory recitative or the virulent harmony of his great master.

At least two pupils came from abroad. One of them was an Englishman, Walter Porter, who, in publishing a book of motets in 1657, proudly pointed out that these were in the Italian style and were the result of his studies in Italy. In a manuscript note found in a copy of this book at Christ Church, Oxford, he tells us that his teacher was Monteverdi himself. What had Porter learned? Undoubtedly the technique of writing *continuo* madrigals and some of the tricks of the trade. In his book of *Madrigals and Ayres* (1632) he displays the ability to write declamatory melodic lines, the expressive use of dissonance and chromaticism, and the various ornaments which were the stock-in-trade of Italian composers. Further than this it is difficult, if not impossible, to find specifically Monteverdian traits. It is true that he occasionally uses that favourite downward leap of a sixth, but instead of expressing the meaning of some passionate poetic phrase, it is nearly always pictorial (to express the idea of 'falling', for example) in an older English tradition. And he is maladroit in his application of ornaments. The sobbing trill is just as likely to occur on the words 'and' or 'of' as on 'love' or 'grief'. The only closer connection with Monteverdi that we may notice is that his madrigals and airs are for the most part old-fashioned, at least for 1632, and follow the forms to be found in Monteverdi's seventh book. But in fact, Porter could have learned everything from even a minor Italian composer.

The other foreigner, Heinrich Schütz, is much more important. By the time of his visit to Monteverdi in Venice in 1628 he was a man of considerable attainments and over forty years old. It was not his first period of study in Italy, for he had come to Venice to work with Giovanni Gabrieli twenty years before. His style was by this time a unique mixture of Italian and German, completely personal in its adaptation of the Venetian church music technique into German usage. All the more remarkable then was his receptiveness in face of the work of Monteverdi. Whether he was a formal pupil of the Italian is not known and is unimportant; what is certain is that he studied Monteverdi's work with the greatest care. He did more than pick up a few tricks of style—though we can find Monteverdi's downward sixth, chromatic changes and astringent harmonies in Schütz's work too.

He studied the very basis of Monteverdi's 'academic philosophy', as we can see from a book by his own pupil, Christoph Bernhard, whose *Kompositionslehre* goes into the theory of the affections in some detail and with some insight. Most especially, since it was Monteverdi's latest invention, the *stile concitato* affected Schütz's attitude. It is no coincidence that a recently discovered German manuscript of the period [1] (probably the earliest German copy of a Monteverdi work) is a score of part of *Tancredi e Clorinda*, complete with a translation. Schütz may not have made this copy himself, but it must have been his interest that gave it its *raison d'être*. In his own music there are passages in this manner, and his motet *Es steh' Gott auf*, in the second part of the *Symphoniae sacrae* (1647), is largely an adaptation of two of Monteverdi's *continuo* madrigals, *Armato il cor* and *Zefiro torna*. Quite apart from details of the new recitative and *arioso* melody which are to be found all over the *concertato* motets which he published after this journey, we find a change of attitude in his religious music which is very Monteverdian. Such works as *Fili mi, Absalom* and *Saul, Saul, was verfolgst du mich?* are full of dramatic force and remind us of the description of Monteverdi's music for the memorial requiem of Cosimo II of Tuscany. Although we have lost Monteverdi's music for this occasion, Schütz's style helps us to fill in the gap.

In a way this influence on German music and especially on German theory was to be more important than the direct influence of Monteverdi's music on his immediate successors. He left no school of composers behind him. Cavalli, Cesti and the rest learned a great deal from the variety of forms in *Poppea* and *Ulisse*: they did not directly imitate them. Monteverdi was by this time a little too old-fashioned for forward-looking composers. He had 'too many scruples' (as Alfred Einstein puts it), that is, he was always a serious-minded composer with his roots in the old academic theories. His influence had passed into the life of music gradually over the years, by giving the ultimate power to technical means which for the most part had been discovered by other people. Hence in an age which had little

[1] Now in possession of the Musachino College of Music. There is a facsimile edition in 'Festschrift Helmut Osthoff' (Tutzing, 1961).

historical sense his progress in the art was taken for granted and soon forgotten. When he died, however, he was revered as a great master. Camberlotti's memoir [1] shows us that. So does Sansovino's guide-book, which, describing the Chapel of the Lombardi in the Frari Church, says that

in the Chapel, with a tomb by Milanesi is buried Claudio Monteverdi, Maestro di Cappella in St Mark's, a great theorist of vocal and instrumental music, famous for his valour and his compositions, of which many were printed.[2]

It was to the learned men, the writers of treatises, that Monteverdi's reputation was entrusted. Naturally their interests were in his theoretical writings, small in extent though they were. Even in his lifetime one writer, Doni, was discussing his work from the academic point of view. And he had one especially valuable thing to offer. Precisely because he was unable to understand the Greek writers clearly, precisely because he was primarily a practical musician, he had tried to realize what the Platonic theorists meant in terms of musical practice. His promised treatise on the Second Practice was to be a very practical book dealing with methods of representation, with details of harmony and rhythm. To reinforce this, his *stile concitato* was an attempt to apply theory to musical idiom in the most lucid way possible. This was worth more than all the vague references to Platonic theory, all the acoustics and arguments about temperament that had filled the Renaissance treatises. It was a line which had a great deal to offer any composer. First Doni, then Schütz's pupil Bernhard, then a number of minor German writers began to speak of 'moving the affections' in terms of specific musical figures. By the eighteenth century this had flowered into a veritable philosophy of music, and Bach's contemporaries such as Scheibe and Mattheson developed a guide to musical invention based on the various emotions of the verbal texts,

[1] Printed in Malipiero, op. cit., pages 50–62.
[2] *Venetia città nobilissima* (1663 ed.), page 195.

which, while certainly more complicated than anything envisaged by Monteverdi, none the less followed up his line of thought.

In this way Monteverdi's work passed into the main stream of musical tradition; and, as so often happens when a composer's ideas are developed rather than imitated by his followers, his music in itself had little interest for the musician and the public. By the early eighteenth century only an historian would have heard of it—and music historians were very few. When Padre Martini was gathering together his library at Bologna, he took care to collect all of Monteverdi's works that he could find, and he read the Artusi-Monteverdi polemic with some attention. Naturally his attention turned to the madrigals which had been criticized for their dissonance, and especially *Cruda Amarilli*. Although interested more in the style of Palestrina and the orthodox church composers of the sixteenth century, he was no dry-as-dust theorist. He saw Monteverdi's point quite clearly even though he thought it better for the young contrapuntist not to imitate him:

The young composer must reflect that the author [Monteverdi] does not use dissonances prohibited by the rules, except for the purposes of expressing the words, and then only in madrigals. And since by common agreement, as consonances are agreeable to the hearing, so dissonances are displeasing, thus it is that these must not be used unless they obey the rules by being suspensions or passing notes, so that they do not become horrible and displeasing. They are used in madrigals because, the parts composed being only sung, and without the accompaniment of any instrument, it was easier for them to be sung perfectly in tune by a few singers than in church music, in which a crowd of singers sings; for in the crowd, as experience teaches us, not all are capable of a just and perfect intonation.[1]

This is true enough, and Martini knew that Monteverdi could write orthodox counterpoint when he chose because he had scored part of the 'Gombert Mass'. But what is interesting is that he printed for the modern reader quotations from two extreme madrigals, full of the

[1] Quoted by H. F. Redlich, *Claudio Monteverdi, I: Das Madrigalwerk* (Berlin, 1932), page 104.

more progressive harmonies. This was equally true of Charles Burney in his *History of Music*. Burney had examined Monteverdi's music in Martini's library and naturally came to look at the novel passages (as they seemed to him). The legend of Monteverdi the revolutionary was now well established:

Monteverde was the first who used double discords, such as the $\frac{9}{4}$, $\frac{9}{7}$, and $\frac{7}{2}$, as well as the flat fifth and the seventh unprepared; and as he was possessed of more genius and science than the Prince of Venosa, his innovations were not merely praised, and then avoided, but abused, and adopted by other composers.[1]

Neither Burney nor Martini had, we may suspect, transcribed much of Monteverdi's music—the Burney transcripts now in the British Museum show a more complete coverage of many other madrigalists. Yet their authority was sufficient for this picture to persist into the nineteenth century, and Monteverdi's apparently revolutionary discoveries were made more prominent still by the appearance of music from the Vespers in Carl von Winterfeld's study of the music of Giovanni Gabrieli, published in 1834. A few personal documents which came to light about the same time did nothing to change this state of affairs. Verdi, thinking out a curriculum for the young composer to follow, recommended a thorough study of counterpoint, but took care to exclude Monteverdi on the grounds that his part-writing was bad.

As late as 1880 it was possible for a conscientious man such as W. S. Rockstro to write (of Monteverdi) in the first edition of Grove's *Dictionary of Music and Musicians*:

Well would it have been for Polyphonic Art, and for his own reputation, also, had he recognized [that his true vocation was dramatic music] sooner. Had he given his attention to Dramatic Music, from the first, the Mass and the Madrigal might, perhaps, have still been preserved in the purity bequeathed to them by Palestrina and Luca Marenzio. As it was, the utter

[1] *A General History of Music*, III (London, 1789), page 235.

demolition of the older School was effected, before the newer one was built upon its ruins: and Monteverde was as surely the destroyer of the first, as he was the founder of the second.

Rockstro certainly knew more than most people about Monteverdi, and had examined the score of *Orfeo* with care and admiration; but he relied on the same old sources—Artusi, Martini and Burney—for his knowledge of the madrigals. As by this time the music of the sixteenth century meant in fact the music of the Roman school, it is not to be wondered at that even scholars could accept this picture of Monteverdi heaving up the very roots of counterpoint and founding the new music single-handed.

Fortunately rescue was at hand. The Swiss historian Burckhardt, John Addington Symonds and a number of other believers in history as a study of culture rather than of politics were at work in the 1860's and 1870's. Painting and literature were their first subjects. Music followed a little later, being more difficult of access. Inspired by this new attitude a number of musicians and historians began researches into the music of the sixteenth and seventeenth centuries. Davari, in charge of the Gonzaga archives at Mantua, was the first to show an interest in Monteverdi. Working on the various papers over many years, he found the huge series of letters which form the principal material for a biographer, together with most of the minor documents which still exist there. Emil Vogel, a more professional music historian, made a wider search and wrote the first biography of any value, after examining documents at Cremona and Venice, as well as looking at and transcribing a great deal of the music.

By this time the music itself was coming back into view. Alongside the new histories and music journals, which the German revival of old music started with such great enthusiasm, were the new editions. *Orfeo* came out in 1881 in an edition by Robert Eitner, and from then until the beginning of the First World War the madrigals and operas were gradually made public again. By the 1920's Monteverdi's music was reasonably well known to scholars, and a number of these made the attempt to revive the various works. *Orfeo* and *L'incoronazione* were given a number of performances, and some years later the Vespers became almost a popular work in the edition of Hans Redlich. The resurgence of Italian nationalism between the wars bore one of its few pleasant fruits in a collected edition, and a number of excellent monographs have appeared in French, English, German and Italian.

Such activity may remind us of the Bach revival of the nineteenth century; yet the modern scholar must regret one thing. Even now the interest in Monteverdi remains on the whole an historical one. The monographs still echo, though more faintly, the opinions of Burney and Martini. The performances are often entrusted to semi-amateur resources or to professionals who treat the music as though it were a phenomenon rather than an experience. Our consolation must be that this once happened to Bach and Handel. Before long Monteverdi may join their company, not as the creator of modern music but simply as a genius.

APPENDICES

APPENDIX A

CALENDAR

(Figures in brackets denote the age at which the person mentioned died)

Year	Age	Life	Contemporary Musicians
1567		Claudio Zuan [Giovanni] Antonio Monteverdi born (baptized May 15) at Cremona, the son of a doctor, Baldassare Monteverdi.	Campian born, Feb. 12; Giacobbi born, Aug.; Vaet dies, Jan. 8. Anerio (F.) 7; Bull *c.* 5; Byrd 24; Caccini *c.* 22; Cavalieri *c.* 27; Corteccia 63; Croce *c.* 10; Dowland 4; Du Caurroy 18; Eccard 14; Ferrabosco (i) 24; Gabrieli (A.) *c.* 57; Gabrieli (G.) *c.* 10; Gesualdo *c.* 7; Guerrero 40; Handl 17; Hassler 3; Ingegneri *c.* 22; Lassus *c.* 35; Le Jeune 39; Luzzaschi *c.* 22; Marenzio 14; Mauduit 10; Merulo 34; de Monte 46; Morley 10; Palestrina *c.* 42; Peri 6; Porta (C.) *c.* 63; Ruffo *c.* 62; Sweelinck 5; Tallis *c.* 62; Tye *c.* 67; Vecchi (Orazio) 17; Victoria *c.* 19; Walther (J.) 77; de Wert 32.
1568	1		Banchieri born, Sept. 3; Rosseter born.
1569	2		
1570	3		Walther (J.) (*c.* 79) dies, March 25.

Year	Age	Life	Contemporary Musicians
1571	4	Maria Domitilla M. (sister) born (baptized May 16).	Corteccia (66) dies, June 7; Praetorius (M.) born, Feb. 15.
1572	5		Certon dies, Feb. 23; Goudimel (*c.* 58) dies, Aug. 27; Tomkins (T.) born.
1573	6	Giulio Cesare M. (brother) born (baptized Jan. 31).	Tye (*c.* 72) dies.
1574	7		White (R.) dies, Nov.; Wilbye born.
1575	8		
1576	9		
1577	10		
1578	11		Agazzari born, Dec. 2.
1579	12	Clara Massimilla M. (sister) born (baptized Jan. 8).	
1580	13		
1581	14	Luca M. (brother) born (baptized Feb. 2).	Farrant dies.
1582	15	*Sacrae cantiunculae* published. M. describes himself on titlepage as a pupil of Ingegneri.	
1583	16	*Madrigali spirituali* published.	Frescobaldi born, Sept.; Gibbons born, Dec.
1584	17	*Canzonette* for three voices published.	
1585	18		Schütz born, Oct. 14; Tallis (*c.* 80) dies, Nov. 23.
1586	19		Gabrieli (A.) (*c.* 76) dies; Schein born, Jan. 20.
1587	20	1st book of madrigals published.	Ruffo (*c.* 82) dies, Feb. 9; Scheidt born, Nov.
1588	21		Ferrabosco (i) (45) dies, Aug. 12.
1589	22	M. visits Milan with a view to obtaining an appointment, but is unsuccessful.	
1590	23	2nd book of madrigals pub-	

Year	Age	Life	Contemporary Musicians
		lished. M. appointed probably in this year to the household of Vincenzo I, Duke of Mantua, as a string-player (*suonatore di viuola*).	
1591	24		Handl (40) dies, July 18.
1592	25	3rd book of madrigals published.	Ingegneri (*c.* 47) dies, July 1; Jenkins born.
1593	26		Agostini (P.) born.
1594	27		Lassus (62) dies, June 14; Palestrina (*c.* 68) dies, Feb. 2.
1595	28	M. accompanies the Duke of Mantua on an expedition to Hungary.	
1596	29		Lawes (H.) born, Jan. 5; de Wert (60) dies, May 6.
1597	30		
1598	31		Crüger born, April 9; Rossi (L.) born.
1599	32	M. marries the singer Claudia Cattaneo, daughter of the string-player Giacomo C., May 20. He accompanies the Duke of Mantua on a visit to Flanders, June.	Guerrero (72) dies, Nov. 8; Marenzio (46) dies, Aug. 22.
1600	33		
1601	34	Francesco M. (son) born (baptized Aug. 27) at Mantua.	Pallavicino dies, May 6; Porta (*c.* 96) dies, May 26.
1602	35	M. appointed *maestro della musica* to the Duke of Mantua, in succession to Pallavicino.	Cavalieri (*c.* 51) dies, March 11; Cavalli born, Feb. 14, Lawes (W.) born, April.
1603	36	Leonora M. (daughter), born (baptized Feb. 20) at Mantua. 4th book of madrigals published.	De Monte (82) dies, July 4; (?) Morley (46) dies.
1604	37	Massimiliano M. (son) born (baptized May 10) at Mantua.	Albert born, July 8; Merulo (71) dies, May 5.

Year	Age	Life	Contemporary Musicians
1605	38	5th book of madrigals published.	Benevoli born, April 19; Carissimi born, April 18; Vecchi (Orazio) (54) dies, Feb. 19.
1606	39		
1607	40	Opera, *La favola d'Orfeo*, produced at the Accademia degl' Invaghiti, Mantua, Feb. (?) 22. M.'s wife dies, Sept. 10. *Scherzi musicali* (first set) published with an introductory essay by Giulio Cesare M., explaining the preface to the 5th book of madrigals.	Luzzaschi (*c.* 62) dies, Sept. 11.
1608	41	Opera, *L'Arianna*, produced at Mantua, May 28. *Il ballo dell' ingrate* performed there, June 4. Guarini's comedy *L'idropica* (with prologue set by M.) performed there, June 2.	
1609	42	Score of *Orfeo* published.	Croce (*c.* 52) dies, May 15; Du Caurroy (60) dies, Aug. 7.
1610	43	6-part Mass and *Vespers* published, with dedication to Pope Paul V.	
1611	44		Eccard (58) dies, autumn; Victoria (*c.* 63) dies, Aug. 27.
1612	45	Vincenzo I, Duke of Mantua dies, Feb. 18, M. dismissed by his successor, Francesco II, July 31. He returns to Cremona. In the autumn he visits Milan, where he conducts a performance of his music.	Hammerschmidt born; Hassler (47) dies, June 8. Gabrieli (G.) (58) dies, Aug. 12.
1613	46	M. appointed *maestro di cappella* at St Mark's, Venice, Aug. 19, in succession to Giulio Cesare Martinengo.	Gesualdo (*c.* 53) dies, Sept. 8.

Year	Age	Life	Contemporary Musicians
1614	47	6th book of madrigals published.	Anerio (F.) (54) dies, Sept. 27; Tunder born.
1615	48		
1616	49	Ballet, *Tirsi e Clori,* performed at Mantua.	Froberger born, *c.* May 18.
1617	50	M. contributes music to Andreini's *sacra rappresentazione, La Maddalena.*	
1618	51	Francesco M. begins to study law at Bologna.	Caccini (*c.* 73) dies, Dec. 10.
1619	52	7th book of madrigals published.	
1620	53	Francesco M. becomes a Carmelite friar.	Campian (53) dies, March 1.
1621	54	Requiem Mass for Cosimo II de' Medici, Grand Duke of Tuscany, performed at Venice, May 25.	Praetorius (50) dies, Feb. 15; Sweelinck (59) dies, Oct. 16.
1622	55		Gastoldi dies.
1623	56	Francesco M. joins the choir of St Mark's, Venice, July 1. *Lamento d'Arianna* published.	Byrd (80) dies, July 4; Cesti born, Aug.; Reinken born, April 27; Rosseter (55) dies, May 5; Weelkes dies, Nov. 30.
1624	57	*Il combattimento di Tancredi e Clorinda* performed at Venice.	
1625	58		Gibbons (42) dies, June 5.
1626	59	Massimiliano M. graduates as a Doctor of Medicine at Bologna, March 16.	Dowland (63) dies, Jan. 21; Legrenzi born, Aug.
1627	60	Comic opera, *La finta pazza Licori,* composed. Massimiliano M. arrested by the Inquisition.	Mauduit (69) dies, Aug. 21.
1628	61	Massimiliano M. acquitted, summer. Intermezzo, *Gli amori di Diana e di Endimione*	Bull (*c.* 65) dies, March 13.

Year	Age	Life	Contemporary Musicians
		performed at Parma, Dec. 13. *Mercurio e Marte* (*torneo*) performed there, Dec. 21.	
1629	62		Agostini (P.) (36) dies, Oct. 3; Giacobbi (61) dies, Feb.
1630	63	Opera, *Proserpina rapita*, produced at Venice. Outbreak of plague in Venice.	Schein (44) dies, Nov. 19.
1631	64	Thanksgiving Mass for the cessation of the plague performed at St Mark's, Venice, Nov. 28.	
1632	65	M. now is a priest. *Scherzi musicali* (second set) published.	Lully born, Nov. 28.
1633	66		Peri (71) dies, Aug. 12.
1634	67		Banchieri (66) dies.
1635	68		D'Anglebert born.
1636	69		
1637	70		Buxtehude born.
1638	71	8th book of madrigals (*Madrigali guerrieri et amorosi*) published.	Pilkington dies; Wilbye (64) dies.
1639	72	*L'Arianna* revived at Venice for the opening of the Teatro di San Moisè, autumn.	
1640	73	*Selva morale e spirituale* published.	Agazzari (61) dies, April 10.
1641	74	Opera, *Le nozze d'Enea con Lavinia*, produced at Venice. Opera, *Il ritorno d'Ulisse in patria*, produced at Venice, Feb. Ballet, *La vittoria d'amore*, performed at Piacenza.	
1642	75	Opera, *L'incoronazione di Poppea*, produced at Venice, autumn.	Bononcini (G. M.) born, Sept.; Gagliano (*c.* 66) dies, Feb. 24.
1643	76	M. visits Cremona and Man-	Frescobaldi (59) dies, March

Appendix A—Calendar

Year	Age	Life	Contemporary Musicians
		tua, May. He returns to Venice and dies there, Nov. 29.	1. Albert 39; Benevoli 38; Bononcini (G. M.) 1; Buxtehude 6; Carissimi 38; Cavalli 41; Cesti 20; Crüger 45; D'Anglebert 8; Froberger 27; Hammerschmidt 32; Jenkins 51; Lawes (H.) 47; Lawes (W.) 41; Legrenzi 17; Lully 11; Reinken 40; Rossi (L.) 45; Scheidt 56; Schütz 58; Tomkins 71; Tunder 29.

APPENDIX B

CATALOGUE OF WORKS

The letter 'M', followed by Roman numerals, indicates the volume in Malipiero's collected edition. The spellings of titles have not been modernized.

(a) SECULAR

DRAMATIC WORKS

La favola d'Orfeo. Opera (Alessandro Striggio). Mantua, 1607. (M.XI.)

L'Arianna. Opera (Ottavio Rinuccini). Mantua, 1608. (Music lost except for the lament, for which see under *Miscellaneous Pieces.*)

Ballo delle ingrate. Ballet (Ottavio Rinuccini). Mantua, 1608. (M.VIII.)

Prologue to *L'idropica.* Comedy with music (Giovanni Battista Guarini). Mantua, 1608. (Music lost.)

Tirsi e Clori. Ballet (Alessandro Striggio). Mantua, 1616. (M.VII.)

Combattimento di Tancredi et Clorinda. Secular oratorio (Torquato Tasso). Venice, 1624. (M.VIII.)

La finta pazza Licori. Comic opera (Giulio Strozzi). 1627. (Music lost.)

Gli amori di Diana e di Endimione. Intermezzo (Ascanio Pio). Parma, 1628. (Music lost.)

Mercurio e Marte. Torneo (Claudio Achillini). Parma, 1628. (Music lost.)

Proserpina rapita. Opera (Giulio Strozzi). Venice, 1630. (Music lost.)

Volgendo il ciel. Ballet. Vienna (?), 1637. (M.VIII.)

Le nozze d'Enea con Lavinia. Opera (Giacomo Badoaro). Venice, 1641. (Music lost.)

Il ritorno d'Ulisse in patria (Giacomo Badoaro). Venice, 1641. (M.XII.)

La vittoria d'amore. Ballet. Piacenza, 1641. (Music lost.)

L'incoronazione di Poppea (Giovanni Francesco Busenello). Venice, 1642. (M. XIII.)

COLLECTIONS

Canzonette a tre voci (1584). (M.X):

Qual si può dir maggiore
Canzonette d'amore
La fiera vista
Raggi, dov'è il mio bene?
Vita de l'alma mia
Io mio martir tengo
Son questi i crespi crini?
Io mi vivea com'aquila
Su su, che'l giorno è fore
Quando sperai del mio servir mercede
Come farò, cuor mio?

Corse a la morte il povero Narciso
Tu ridi sempre mai
Chi vuol veder d'inverno un dolce aprile
Già mi credev'un sol esser in cielo
Godi pur del bel sen felice
Giù li a quel petto giace
Sì come crescon alla terra i fiori
Io son fenice e voi sete la fiamma
Chi vuol veder un bosco
Hor, care canzonette

Il primo libro de madrigali a cinque voci (1587). (M.I):

Ch'io ami la mia vita
Se per haverui oimè
A che tormi il ben mio?
Amor per tua mercè vatene a quella
Baci soavi e cari (Guarini)
Se pur non mi consenti
Filli cara e amata
Poi che del mio dolore
{ Fumia la pastorella (1ª parte)
{ Almo divino raggio (2ª parte)
{ All'hora i pastor tutti (3ª parte)
    (Allegretti)
Se nel partir da voi, vita mia

Tra mille fiamme e tra mille cathene
Usciam, ninfe, homai fuor di questi
    boschi
Questa ordì il laccio (Strozzi)
La vaga pastorella sen va tra fiori
Amor, s'il tuo ferire
Donna, s'io miro voi, giaccio divengo
Ardo, sì, ma non t'amo (Guarini)
Ardi o gela a tua voglia (Risposta)
    (Tasso)
Arsi e alsi a mia voglia (Contra-
    risposta) (Tasso)

Il secondo libro de madrigali a cinque voci (1590). (M.II):

{ Non si levav'ancor l'alba novella
{   (1ª parte)
{ E dicea l'una sospirando (2ª parte)
    (Tasso)
Bevea Fillide mia (Casoni)
Dolcissimi legami di parole amorose
    (Tasso)

Non giacinti o narcisi (Casoni)
Intorno a due vermiglie e vaghe labra
Non sono in queste rive fiori così
    vermigli (Tasso)
Tutte le bocche belle in questo nero
    volto (Alberti)
Donna, nel mio ritorno (Tasso)

Quell'ombra esser vorrei (Casoni)
S'andasse amor a caccia (Tasso)
Mentre io miravo fiso de la mia donna
gl'occh'ardenti e belli (Tasso)
Se tu mi lassi, perfida (Tasso)
Ecco mormorar l'onde (Tasso)
La bocc'onde l'asprissime parole solean
uscir (Bentivoglio)
Dolcemente dormiva la mia Clori
(Tasso)

Crudel, perchè mi fuggi? (Tasso)
Questo specchio ti dono, Rosa
Non m'è grave'l morire
Ti spontò l'ali amor, la donna mia
(Alberti)
Cantai un tempo, e se fu dolc'il canto
(Bembo)

Il terzo libro de madrigali a cinque voci (1592). (M.III):

La giovinetta pianta si fa più bell'al
sole
O come è gran martire (Guarini)
Sovra tenere herbette e bianchi fiori
O dolce anima mia (Guarini)
Stracciami pur il core (Guarini)
O rossignol ch'in queste verdi fronde
(Bembo)
Se per estremo ardore morir potesse
un core (Guarini)
⎧ *Vattene pur, crudel, con quella pace*
⎪ (1ª *parte*)
⎨ *Là tra'l sangu'e le morti* (2ª *parte*)
⎪ *Poi ch'ella in sè tornò* (3ª *parte*)
⎩ (Tasso)
O primavera, gioventù de l'anno
(Guarini)

Perfidissimo volto (Guarini)
Ch'io non t'ami, cor mio (Guarini)
Occhi un tempo, mia vita, occhi di
questo cor fido sostegno (Guarini)
⎧ *Vivrò fra i miei tormenti e le mie cure*
⎪ (1ª *parte*)
⎨ *Ma dove, o lasso me, dove restaro?*
⎪ (2ª *parte*)
⎪ *Io pur verrò là dove sete* (3ª *parte*)
⎩ (Tasso)
Lumi miei, cari lumi (Guarini)
⎧ *Rimanti in pace a la dolente e bella*
⎪ *Fillida* (1ª *parte*)
⎨ *Ond'ei di morte la sua faccia impresa*
⎩ (2ª *parte*) (Celiano)

Il quarto libro de madrigali a cinque voci (1603). (M.IV):

Ah dolente partita (Guarini)
Cor mio, mentre vi miro (Guarini)
Cor mio, non mori?
Sfogava con le stelle un inferno
d'amore (Rinuccini)
Volgea l'anima mia soavemente
(Guarini)

⎧ *Anima mia, perdona* (1ª *parte*)
⎨ *Che se tu se'il cor mio* (2ª *parte*)
⎩ (Guarini)
Luci serene e chiare, voi m'incendete
La piaga c'ho nel core
Voi pur da me partite, anima dura
(Guarini)

180

A un giro sol de' bell'ochi lucenti
(Guarini)
Obimè, se tanto amate di sentir dir
obimè (Guarini)
Io mi son giovinetta (Boccaccio)
Quel augellin che canta si dolcemente
(Boccaccio)

Non più guerra, pietate (Guarini)
Sì ch'io vorrei morire
Anima dolorosa
Anima del cor mio
Longe da te, cor mio, struggomi di
dolore
Piagne e sospira

Il quinto libro de madrigali a cinque voci (1605). (M.V):

Cruda Amarilli (Guarini)
O Mirtillo, Mirtill'anima mia
(Guarini)
Era l'anima mia già presso a l'ultim'
bore (Guarini)
{ Ecco, Silvio, colei ch'in odio hai tanto
(1ᵃ parte)
Ma se con la pietà non è in te spenta
(2ᵃ parte)
Dorinda, ah dirò mia, se mia non sei
(3ᵃ parte)
Ecco piegando le ginocchie a terra
(4ᵃ parte)
Ferir quel petto, Silvio (5ᵃ parte)
(Guarini)

{ Ch'io t'ami e t'ami più de la mia vita
(1ᵃ parte)
Deh, bella e cara (2ᵃ parte)
Ma tu più che mai dura (3ᵃ parte)
(Guarini)
Che dar più vi poss'io ?
M'è più dolce il penar per Amarilli
(Guarini)
Abi, com'a un vago sol cortese giro
Troppo ben può questo tiranno amore
(Guarini)
Amor, se giusto sei
T'amo, mia vita (Guarini)
E così a poc'a poco torno farfalla (a
sei voci) (Guarini)
Questi vaghi concenti (a nove voci)

Scherzi musicali a tre voci . . . raccolti da Giulio Cesare Monteverde [1] (1607).
(M.X):

I bei legami (Chiabrera)
Amarilli onde m'assale (Chiabrera)
Fugge il verno dei dolori (Chiabrera)
Quando l'alba in oriente (Chiabrera)
Non così tosto io miro (Chiabrera)
Damigella tutta bella (Chiabrera)
La pastorella mia spietata (Sanna-
zaro)

O rosetta, che rosetta (Chiabrera)
Amorosa pupilletta
Vaghi rai di cigli ardenti (Chiabrera)
La violetta (Chiabrera)
Giovinetta ritrosetta
Dolci miei sospiri (Chiabrera)
Clori amorosa (Chiabrera)
Lidia, spina del mio core

---

[1] *Deh, chi tace il ben pensero* (Cebà) and *Dispiegate, guance amate* (Cebà),
included in this collection, are by Giulio Cesare Monteverdi. The composer of
the *balletto* which ends the collection, *De la bellezza le dovute lodi*, is uncertain.

Monteverdi

Il sesto libro de madrigali a cinque voci, con uno Dialogo a Sette (1614). (M.VI):

Lamento d'Arianna [1] (Rinuccini):
  Lasciatemi morire (1ª parte)
  O Teseo, Teseo mio (2ª parte)
  Dove, dove è la fede (3ª parte)
  Ahi, ch'ei non pur risponde (4ª
    (parte
Zefiro torna e'l bel tempo rimena
  (Petrarch)
Una donna fra l'altre honesta e bello
  vidi (concertato nel clavicembalo)
A Dio, Florida bella (concertato)
  (Marini)
Batto qui pianse Ergasto (concertato
  nel clavicembalo) (Marini)
Presso un fiume tranquillo (dialogo a
  7, concertato) (Marini)

Sestina (Lagrime d'amante al sepolcro
  dell'amata) (Agnelli):
  Incenerite spoglie, avara tomba (1ª
    parte)
  Ditelo, o fiumi e voi ch'udiste (2ª
    parte)
  Darà la notte il sol (3ª parte)
  Ma te raccoglie, o ninfa (4ª parte)
  O chiome d'or, neve gentil del seno
    (5ª parte)
  Dunque amate reliquie (6ª parte)
Ohimè, il bel viso (Petrarch)
Qui rise Tirsi (concertato) (Marini)
Misero Alceo (concertato)

Concerto. *Settimo libro de madrigali a 1. 2. 3. 4. & 6. voci, con altri generi de canti* (1619). (M.VII):

Tempro la cetra (T., with *sinfonia* and *ritornelli* for 5-part str.) (Marini)
Non è di gentil core chi non arde (S.S.)
  (Degl'Atti)
A quest'olmo, a quest'ombre (a sei
  voci, concertato, with 2 vlns. & 2
  recorders or fl.) (Marini)
O come sei gentile, caro augellino
  (S.S.) (Guarini)
Io son pur vezzosetta pastorella
  (S.S.)

Dice la mia bellissima Licori (T.T.)
  (Guarini)
Ah, che non si conviene romper la
  fede? (T.T.)
Non vedrò mai le stelle (T.T.)
Ecco vicine, o bella tigre, l'hore (T.T.)
O viva fiamma, o miei sospiri ardenti
  (S.S.)
Vorrei baciarti, o Filli (A.A.)
  (Marini)

---

[1] Arranged by the composer from the only surviving fragment of the opera *L'Arianna* (see under *Miscellaneous Pieces*).

Perchè fuggi tra salci, ritrosetta? (T.T.) (Marini)

Tornate, o cari baci (T.T.) (Marini)

Soave libertate (T.T.) (Chiabrera)

S'el vostro cor, madonna (T.B.) (Guarini)

Interrotte speranze (T.T.) (Guarini)

Augellin, che la voce al canto spieghi (T.T.B.)

Vaga su spina ascosa (T.T.B.) (Chiabrera)

Eccomi pronta ai baci, Ergasto mio (T.T.B.) (Marini)

Parlo, miser, o taccio? (S.S.B.) (Guarini)

Tu dormi? Ah crudo core (S.A.T.B.)

Al lume delle stelle (S.S.T.B.)

Con che soavità, labbra odorate (*concertato a una voce* [S.] *e 9 istrumenti* [str., lutes, harpsichords, organ]) (Guarini)

Ohimè, dov'è il mio ben? (1^a *parte*)

Dunque ha potuto sol desio d'honore (2^a *parte*)

Dunque ha potuto in me più che'l mio amore (3^a *parte*)

Ahi sciocco mondo e cieco (4^a *parte*) (*Romanesca a 2* [S.S.]) (Bernardo Tasso)

Se i languidi miei sguardi (*Lettera amorosa a voce sola* [S.])

Se pur destina e vole il cielo (*Partenza amorosa a voce sola* [T.])

Chiome d'oro, bel thesoro (*Canzonetta a due voci* [S.S.] *concertata da duoi violini, chitarone o spineta*)

Amor che deggio far? (*Canzonetta a 4* [S.S.T.B.] *concertato come di sopra,* [2 vlns. & lute or harpsichord])

Tirsi e Clori (*Ballo*) (see *Dramatic Works*)

Scherzi musicali Cioè Arie, & Madrigali in stil recitativo, con una Ciaccona a 1. & 2. voci . . . Raccolti da Bartholomeo Magni (1632). (M.X):

Maledetto sia l'aspetto (S.)

Quel sguardo sdegnosetto (S.)

Armatevi, pupille (S.)

Begli occhi, all'armi (S.)

Eri già tutta mia (S.)

Ecco di dolci raggi (T.)

Et è pur dunque vero (*a voce sola* [S.] *con sinfonie* [vln.?])

Io che armato sin hor (T.)

Zefiro torna (*Ciacona a 2* [T.T.]) (Rinuccini) (M.IX)

Armato il cor d'adamantina fede (T.T.) (M.IX)

Madrigali guerrieri et amorosi con alcuni opuscoli in genere rappresentativo, che saranno per brevi Episodii frà i canti senza gesto. Libro ottavo (1638). (M.VIII):

Canti guerrieri

Altri canti d'amor (a 6 voci con quatro viole e duoi violini)

Hor che'l ciel e la terra e'l vento tace (1ᵃ parte)

Così sol d'una chiara fonte viva (2ᵃ parte)

(a 6 voci con duoi violini) (Petrarch)

Gira il nemico insidioso (1ᵃ parte)

Nol lasciamo accostar (2ᵃ parte)

Armi false non son (3ᵃ parte)

Vuol degl'occhi attaccar il baloardo (4ᵃ parte)

Non è più tempo, ohimè (5ᵃ parte)

Cor mio, non val fuggir (6ᵃ parte) (A.T.B.)

Se vittorie sì belle (T.T.) (M.IX.)

Armato il cor d'adamantina fede (T.T.) (M.IX)

Ogni amante è guerrier (1ᵃ parte) (T.T.)

Io che nell'otio naqui e d'otio vissi (2ᵃ parte) (B.)

Ma per quel ampio Egeo spieghi le vele (3ᵃ parte) (T.)

Riedi ch'al nostr'ardir (4ᵃ parte) (T.T.B.)

Ardo, avvampo, mi struggo (a 8, con doi violini)

Combattimento di Tancredi et Clorinda (Tasso) (see *Dramatic Works*)

Volgendo il ciel (Ballo) (see *Dramatic Works*)

Canti amorosi

Altri canti di Marte (1ᵃ parte)

Due belli occhi fur l'armi (2ᵃ parte)

(a 6 voci et doi violini) (Marini)

Vago augelletto, che cantando vai (a 6 et 7 voci con doi violini e un contrabasso) (Petrarch)

Mentre vaga Angioletta ogn'anima gentil cantando alletta (T.T.) (Guarini)

Ardo, e scoprir, ahi lasso, io non ardisco (T.T.)

O sia tranquillo il mare (T.T.)

Ninfa che scalza il piede (1ᵃ parte) (T.)

Qui, deh, meco t'arresta (2ᵃ parte) (T.T.)

Dell'usate mie corde al suon (3ᵃ parte) (T.T.B.)

Dolcissimo uscignolo (a 5 voci, cantato a voce piena, alla francese) (Guarini)

Chi vol haver felice e lieto il core (a 5 voci, cantato a voce piena, alla francese) (Guarini)

Non havea Febo ancora (1ᵃ parte) (T.T.B.)

Amor, dicea (Lamento della ninfa) (2ᵃ parte) (S.T.T.B.)

Sì tra sdegnosi pianti (3ᵃ parte) (T.T.B.) (Rinuccini)

Perchè t'en fuggi, o Fillide? (A.T.B.)

Non partir, ritrosetta (A.A.B.)

Su su, pastorelli vezzosi (S.S.A.)

Ballo delle ingrate (in genere rappresentativo) (see *Dramatic Works*)

Appendix B—Catalogue of Works

Madrigali e canzonette a due e tre voci . . . Libro nono (1651). (M.IX):

Bel pastor dal cui bel guardo (S.T.)
(Rinuccini)

Zefiro torna (T.T.) (Rinuccini)[1]

Se vittorie si belle (T.T.)[2]

Armato il cor d'adamantina fede
(T.T.)[3]

Ardo, e scoprir, ahi lasso, io non
ardisco (T.T.)[2]

O sia tranquillo il mare (T.T.)[2]

Alcun non mi consigli (A.T.B.)

Di far sempre gioire amor speranza
dà (A.T.B.)

Quando dentro al tuo seno (T.T.B.)

Non voglio amare per non penare
(T.T.B.)

Come dolce hoggi l'auretta spira
(S.S.S.)

Alle danze, alle gioie (T.T.B.)

Perchè se m'odiavi (T.T.B.)

Si si ch'io v'amo, occhi vagi, occhi
belli (T.T.T.)

Su su, pastorelli vezzosi (T.T.B.)

O mio bene, o mia vita (T.T.B.)

MISCELLANEOUS PIECES

Lamento d'Arianna . . . Et con due Lettere Amorose in genere rappresentativo (1623):

Lasciatemi morire (S.)[4] (M.XI)

Se i languidi miei sguardi (S.)[5] (M.VII)

Se pur destina e vole il cielo (T.)[5] (M.VII)

In *Il primo libro delle Canzonette a tre voci, di Antonio Morsolino con alcune altre
de diversi Eccellenti Musici* (1594):

Io ardo, sì, ma'l fuoco di tal sorte
(S.S.B.)[6]

Occhi miei, se mirar, più non debb'io
(S.S.B.)[6]

Quante son stelle in ciel (S.S.B.)
(Cerreto)[6]

Se non mi date aita (S.S.B.)[6]

---

[1] Previously published in *Scherzi musicali* (1632).

[2] Previously published in *Madrigali guerrieri et amorosi* (1638).

[3] Previously published in *Scherzi musicali* (1632) and *Madrigali guerrieri
et amorosi* (1638).

[4] An extract from the lost opera *L'Arianna*. There are several manuscript
copies. For the madrigal version see page 182, *Il sesto libro de madrigali*.

[5] Previously published in *Concerto. Settimo libro de madrigali* (1619).

[6] Printed in W. Osthoff, *12 composizioni vocali profane e sacre (inedite)* (1958).

Monteverdi

In *I Nuovi Fioretti Musicali a tre voci d'Amante Franzoni Mantovano* . . .
Raccolti dall'illustrissimo Signor Fulvio Gonzaga marchese (1605):

    Prima vedrò ch'in questi prati (S.S.B.) [1]

In *Madrigali del Signor Cavaliere Anselmi* . . . *posti in musica da diversi eccellentissimi spiriti* (1624):

    O come vaghi, o come cari (T.T.) (M.IX)
    Taci, Armelin, deh taci (A.T.B.) (M.IX)

In *Quarto Scherzo delle ariose vaghezze, commode da cantarsi à voce sola* . . . *di
Carlo Milanuzzi* . . . *con una cantata, & altre arie del Signor Monteverde, e
del Sig. Francesco suo figliolo* (1624) [2]:

    Ohimè ch'io cado, ohimè ch'inciampo (M.IX)
    La mia turca che d'amor (M.IX)
    Si dolce è'l tormento (M.IX)

In *Arie de diversi raccolte da Alessandro Vincenti* (1634):

    Più lieto il guardo (S.) [3]
    Perchè, se m'odiavi (S.) [3]

Surviving in manuscript:

    Ahi, che si partì il mio bel sol adorno (S.S.T.) [4] (M.XVI):
    Lamento d'Olimpia (S.) [5]:
      Voglio morir: van'è'l conforto tuo (1^a *parte*)
      Anzi che non amarmi (2^a *parte*)
      Ma perchè, o ciel, invendicate lassi (3^a *parte*)
    Voglio di vita uscir (S.) [6]

---

[1] Printed in Osthoff, op. cit.

[2] The only known copy of this collection was formerly in the Hamburg
Staats- und Universitätsbibliothek.

[3] Printed in D. De' Paoli, *Claudio Monteverdi* (1945).

[4] Modena, Biblioteca Estense.

[5] British Museum, Add. 30491. Printed in Osthoff, op. cit.

[6] Naples, Archivio dei Filippini, S.M.-IV-2-23b. Printed in Osthoff,
op. cit.

(b) SACRED

DRAMATIC WORKS

Prologue to *La Maddalena*. *Sacra rappresentazione* (Giovanni Battista Andreini). 1617. (See under *Miscellaneous Pieces*.)

COLLECTIONS

Sacrae cantiunculae tribus vocibus . . . Liber primus (1582). (M.XIV):

Lapidabant Stephanum

Veni in hortum meum

Ego sum pastor bonus

Surge propera, amica mea

Ubi duo vel tres congregati fuerint

Quam pulchra es

Ave Maria, gratia plena

Domine Pater et Deus vitae meae

{ Tu es pastor ovium (1ᵃ pars)

{ Tu es Petrus (2ᵃ pars)

{ O magnum pietatis opus (1ᵃ pars)

{ 'Eli' clamans (2ᵃ pars)

O crux benedicta

Hodie Christus natus est

{ O Domine Jesu Christe (1ᵃ pars)

{ O Domine Jesu Christe (2ᵃ pars)

Pater, venit hora

In tua patientia

Angelus ad pastores ait

Salve, crux pretiosa

Quia vidisti me, Thoma, credidisti

Lauda, Sion, Salvatorem

O bone Jesu, illumina oculos meos

Surgens Jesus, Dominus noster

Qui vult venire post me

Iusti tulerunt spolia impiorum

Madrigali spirituali a quattro voci (1583) [1] (M.XVI):

Sacrosanta di Dio verace imago

{ Laura del ciel sempre feconda (1ᵃ parte)

{ Poi che benigno il novo cant' attende (2ᵃ parte)

{ Aventurosa notte (1ᵃ parte)

{ Serpe crudel (2ᵃ parte)

{ D'empi martiri (1ᵃ parte)

{ Ond'in ogni pensier (2ᵃ parte)

{ Mentre la stell'appar (1ᵃ parte)

{ Tal contra Dio de la superbia il corno (2ᵃ parte)

{ Le rose, gli amaranti e gigli (1ᵃ parte)

{ Ai piedi havendo (2ᵃ parte)

{ L'empio vestia di porpora (1ᵃ parte)

{ Ma quel medico (2ᵃ parte)

{ L'human discorso (1ᵃ parte)

{ L'eterno Dio quel cor pudico scelse (2ᵃ parte)

{ Dal sacro petto esce veloce dardo (1ᵃ parte)

{ Scioglier m'addita (2ᵃ parte)

{ Afflitto e scalz'ove la sacra sponda (1ᵃ parte)

{ Ecco, dicea (2ᵃ parte)

{ Dei miei giovenil anni (1ᵃ parte)

{ Tutt'esser vidi (2ᵃ parte)

---

[1] A single copy of the bass part only survives at Bologna, Biblioteca di Conservatorio.

Monteverdi

Sanctissimae Virgini Missa senis vocibus ad ecclesiarum choros Ac Vespere pluribus decantandae cum nonnullis sacris concentibus ad Sacella sive Principum Cubicula accommodata (1610). (M.XIV):

Missa de Cappella a sei voci, fatta sopra il motetto 'In illo tempore' del Gomberti :

    Kyrie eleison
    Et in terra pax
    Patrem omnipotentem
    Sanctus
    Agnus Dei

Vespro della Beata Vergine (da con-certo, composto sopra canti fermi sex vocibus et sex instrumentis) :

    Domine ad adiuvandum (6 v., 2 cornetts, 3 tromb. & 6-part str.)
    Dixit Dominus (sex vocibus et sex instrumentis)
    Nigra sum sed formosa (T.)
    Laudate, pueri, Dominum (a 8 voci sole nel organo)

Pulchra es, amica mea (S.S.)
Laetatus sum (a 6 voci)
Duo Seraphim clamabant (T.T.T.)
Nisi Dominus aedificaverit domum (a 10 voci)
Audi, coelum, verba mea (T. & chorus *a 6 voci*)
Lauda, Jerusalem, Dominum (a 7 voci)
Sonata sopra Sancta Maria, ora pro nobis (S. with 2 cornetts, 3 tromb., 2 vlns. & cello)
Ave maris stella (a 8, a 4, S.T., with 5-part *ritornelli*)
Magnificat (7 v., 2 fl., 2 recorders, 3 cornetts, 2 tromb., 2 vlns. & cello)
Magnificat (a 6 voci, with organ)

Selva morale e spirituale (1640). (M.XV. 1 & 2):

O ciechi il tanto affaticar che giova (a 5 voci et doi violini)
Voi ch'ascoltate in rime sparse (id.)
È questa vita un lampo (a 5 voci)
Spuntava il dì (Canzonetta morale, A.T.B.)
Chi vol che m'innamori (A.T.B., with 3-part str. *ritornello*)
Messa a 4 da Cappella :
    Kyrie eleison
    Et in terra pax
    Patrem omnipotentem

    Sanctus
    Agnus Dei
Gloria in excelsis Deo (a 7 voci concertata con due violini et quattro viole de brazzo overo 4 Tromboni)
Crucifixus (1ª pars) (A.T.T.B., concertato con quattro Tromboni o viole da brazzo)[1]
Et resurrexit (2ª pars) (S.S. or T.T., 2 vlns.)[1]
Et iterum venturus est (3ª pars) (A.A.B.)[1]

---

[1] These three pieces are alternatives to the corresponding sections of the *Messa a 4 da Cappella.*

Ab aeterno ordinata sum (B.)

Dixit Dominus Domino meo (I) (*a 8 voci concertato con due violini et quattro viole o Tromboni*)

Dixit Dominus Domino meo (II) (id.)

Confitebor tibi, Domine (I) (*a 3 voci con 5 altre voci ne ripieni*)

Confitebor tibi, Domine (II) (S.T.B., 2 vlns.)

Confitebor tibi, Domine (III) (*alla francese, a 5 voci or S. & 4-part str.*)

Beatus vir (I) (*a 6 voci concertato con due violini et 3 viole da brazzo ovvero 3 Tromboni*)

Beatus vir (II) (*a 5 voci*)

Laudate, pueri, Dominum (I) (*a 5 concertato con due violini*)

Laudate, pueri, Dominum (II) (*a 5 voci*)

Laudate Dominum, omnes gentes (I) (*a 5 voci concertato con due violini et un choro a quattro voci . . . con quattro viole o Tromboni*)

Laudate Dominum, omnes gentes (II) (*a 8 voci et due violini*)

Laudate Dominum, omnes gentes (III) (*a 8 voci*)

Credidi propter quod locutus sum (*a 8 voci da Cappella*)

Memento, [Domine, David] et omnis mansuetudinis eius (id.)

Sanctorum meritis inclita gaudia (I) (S., 2 vlns.)

Sanctorum meritis inclita gaudia (II) (T., 2 vlns.) [1]

Deus tuorum militum sors et corona (id.) [1]

Iste confessor Domini sacratus (I) (id.) [1]

Iste confessor Domini sacratus (II) (S.S., 2 vlns.) [2]

Ut queant laxis resonare fibris (id.) [2]

Deus tuorum militum sors et corona (A.T.B., 2 vlns.)

Magnificat (I) (*a 8 voci et due violini et quattro viole overo quattro Tromboni*)

Magnificat (II) (*a quattro voci in genere da Capella*)

Salve Regina (I) (T.T. [echo], 2 vlns.)

Salve Regina (II) (T.T. or S.S.)

Salve Regina (III) (A.T. [or S.] B.)

Jubilet tota civitas (S.)

Laudate Dominum in sanctis eius (S. or T.)

Iam moriar, mi Fili (*Pianto della Madonna sopra il Lamento d'Arianna*) (S.) [3]

---

[1] These three pieces are set to the same music.

[2] These two pieces are set to the same music.

[3] An adaptation to sacred words of the solo *Lasciatemi morire* from the opera *L'Arianna*.

Messa a quattro voci, et Salmi A Una, Due, Tre, Quattro, Cinque, Sei, Sette, & Otto Voci, Concertati, e Parte da Cappella, & con le Letanie della B.V. (1650). (M.XVI):

Messa a 4 voci da Cappella :
   Kyrie eleison
   Et in terra pax
   Patrem omnipotentem
   Sanctus
   Agnus Dei
Dixit Dominus Domino meo (I) (8 v.)
Dixit [Dominus Domino meo] (II) (*a 8 voci, alla breve*)
Confitebor tibi, Domine (I) (S., 2 vlns.)
Confitebor tibi, Domine (II) (S.T., 2 vlns.)
Beatus vir (*a 7 voci con 2 violini*)
Laudate, pueri, Dominum (*a 5 voci da Cappella*)

Laudate Dominum, O omnes gentes (B.)
Laetatus sum (I) (6 v., bassoon, 2 tromb., 2 vlns.)
Laetatus sum (II) (*a 5 voci*)
Nisi Dominus aedificaverit domum (I) (S.T.B., 2 vlns.)
Nisi Dominus aedificaverit domum (II) (*a 6 voci*)
Lauda, Jerusalem, Dominum (I) (A.T.B.)
Lauda, Jerusalem, Dominum (II) (*a 5 voci*)
Laetaniae della Beata Vergine (*a 6 voci*)

MISCELLANEOUS PIECES

In *Parnassus musicus Ferdinandeus . . . a Joanne Baptista Bonometti . . . congestus* (1615):

   Cantate Domino canticum novum (S.S. or T.T.) (M.XVI)

In *Musiche de alcuni eccellentissimi musici composte per la Maddalena sacra rappresentazione di Gio. Battista Andreini fiorentino* (1617):

   Su le penne de' venti (T., with 5-part *ritornello*) (M.XI)

In *Symbolae diversorum musicorum . . . Ab admodum reverendo D. Laurentio Calvo . . . in lucem editae* (1620):

   Fuge, anima mea, mundum (S.A., vln.) (M.XVI)
   O beatae viae, O felices gressus (S.S.) (M.XVI)

In *Libro primo de motetti . . . di Giulio Cesare Bianchi. Con un altro a cinque, e tre a sei del sig. Claudio Monteverde* (1620):

> Cantate Domino canticum novum (*a 6 voci*) (M.XVI)
> Christe, adoramus te (*a 5 voci*) (M.XVI)
> Domine, ne in furore tuo arguas me (*a 6 voci*) (M.XVI)
> Adoramus te, Christe (*a 6 voci*) (M.XVI)

In *Promptuarii musici concentus ecclesiasticos II. III. et IV. vocum . . . e diversis, iisque illustrissimis et musica laude praestantissimis hujus aetatis authoribus, collectos exhibentis. Pars prima . . . Collectore Joanne Donfrido* (1622):

> O bone Jesu, O piissime Jesu (S.S.) (M.XVI)

In *Seconda raccolta de' sacri canti . . . de diversi eccellentissimi autori fatta da Don Lorenzo Calvi* (1624):

> Ego flos campi et lilium convallium (A.) (M.XVI)
> Venite siccientes ad aquas Domini (S.S.) (M.XVI)
> Salve, O Regina, O Mater (T.) (M.XVI)

In *Sacri affetti con testi da diversi eccellentissimi autori raccolti da Francesco Sammaruco* (1625):

> Ego dormio et cor meum vigilat (S.B.) (M.XVI)

In *Ghirlanda sacra scielta da diversi eccellentissimi compositori de varii motetti à voce sola. Libro primo opera seconda per Leonardo Simonetti* (1625):

> O quam pulchra es, amica mea (T.) (M.XVI)
> Currite, populi, psallite timpanis (T.) (M.XVI)
> Ecce sacrum paratum convivium (T.) (M.XVI)
> Salve Regina (T.) (M.XVI)

In *Promptuarii musici concentus ecclesiasticos CCLXXXVI selectissimos, II. III. & IV. vocum . . . exhibens, pars tertia . . . Opera et studio Joannis Donfrid* (1627):

> Sancta Maria, succurre miseris (S.S.) (M.XVI)

In *Psalmi de Vespere a quattro voci del Cavalier D. Gio. Maria Sabino da Turi* (1627):

> Confitebor tibi, Domine (*a 4 voci*) [1]

---

[1] Printed in W. Osthoff, *12 composizioni vocali profane e sacre (inedite)* (1958).

In *Quarta raccolta de sacri canti . . . de diversi eccellentissimi autori, fatta da Don Lorenzo Calvi* (1629):

> *Exulta, filia Sion* (S.) [1]
> *Exultent caeli et gaudeant angeli* (*a 5 voci*) [1]

In *Motetti a voce sola da diversi eccellentissimi autori . . . Libro primo* (1645):

> *Venite, videte martyrem quam sit carus* (S.) [1]

In *Raccolta di motetti a 1, 2, 3 voci di Gasparo Casati et de diversi altri eccellentissimi autori* (1651):

> *En gratulemur hodie* (T., 2 vlns.) (M.XVI)

Surviving in manuscript:

> *Gloria in excelsis Deo* (*a 8 voci*) [2]

MADRIGALS ADAPTED TO SACRED TEXTS

(Figures in brackets refer to the number of the madrigal book in which the original occurs)

In *Musica tolta da i madrigali di Claudio Monteverde, e d'altri autori, a cinque, et a sei voci, e fatta spirituale da Aquilino Coppini* (1607):

Felle amaro	=	*Cruda Amarilli* (5)
Gloria tua	=	*T'amo, mia vita* (5)
Maria, quid ploras ?	=	*Dorinda, ah dirò mia* (5)
Pulchrae sunt	=	*Ferir quel petto* (5)
Qui pependit	=	*Ecco, Silvio* (5)
Sancta Maria	=	*Deh, bella e cara* (5)
Spernit Deus	=	*Ma tu più che mai dura* (5)
Stabat Virgo	=	*Era l'anima mia* (5)
Te, Jesu Christe	=	*Ecco piegando* (5)
Ure me	=	*Troppo ben può* (5)
Vives in corde	=	*Ahi, com'a un vago sol* (5)

---

[1] Printed in W. Osthoff, *12 composizioni vocali profane e sacre* (*inedite*) (1958).

[2] Naples, Archivio dei Filippini, S.M.-IV-2-23a. Printed in Osthoff, op. cit.

Appendix B—Catalogue of Works

In *Il secondo libro della musica di Claudio Monteverde e d'altri autori à 5 voci fatta spirituale da Aquilino Coppini* (1608):

Animas eruit	=	*M'è più dolce il penar* (5)
Florea serta	=	*La giovinetta pianta* (3)
O dies infelices	=	*O come è gran martire* (3)
O infelix recessus	=	*Ah dolente partita* (4)
O mi Fili	=	*O Mirtillo* (5)
Praecipitantur, Jesu Christe	=	*O primavera* (3)
Qui regnas	=	*Che dar più vi poss'io ?* (5)
Te sequar	=	*Ch'io t'ami* (5)

In *Il terzo libro della musica di Claudio Monteverde . . . fatta spirituale da Aquilino Coppini* (1609):

Amemus te	=	*Amor, se giusto sei* (5)
Anima miseranda	=	*Anima dolorosa* (4)
Anima quam dilexi	=	*Anima del cor mio* (4)
Ardebat igne	=	*Volgea l'anima mea* (4)
Cantemus	=	*A un giro sol* (4)
Domine Deus	=	*Anima mia, perdona* (4)
Jesu, dum te	=	*Cor mio, mentre vi miro* (4)
Jesu, tu obis	=	*Cor mio, non mori ?* (4)
Longe a te	=	*Longe da te, cor mio* (4)
O gloriose martyr	=	*Che se tu se'il cor mio* (4)
O Jesu, mea vita	=	*Si ch'io vorrei morire* (4)
O stellae	=	*Sfogava con le stelle* (4)
Plagas tuas	=	*La piaga c'ho nel core* (4)
Plorat amare	=	*Piagn'e sospira* (4)
Qui laudes	=	*Quel augellin che canta* (4)
Qui pietate	=	*Ma se con la pietà* (5)
Rutilante in nocte	=	*Io mi son giovinetta* (4)
Tu vis a me	=	*Voi pur da me partite* (4)
Una es [1]	=	*Una donna fra l'altre* (6)

In *Concerti sacri . . . libro secondo . . . del P. Pietro Lappi* (1623):

Ave regina mundi	=	*Vaga su spina ascosa* (7)

---

[1] Published five years before the original madrigal.

Monteverdi

In Erster Theil geistlicher Concerten und Harmonien a 1. 2. 3. 4. 5. 6. 7. &c.
vocibus ... ausz den berühmbsten italienischen und andern Autoribus ... colligiret
... durch Ambrosium Profum (1641):

Jesum viri senesque   = Vaga su spina ascosa (7)

In Ander Theil geistlicher Concerten und Harmonien ... colligiret ... durch
Ambrosium Profum (1641):

Ergo gaude, laetare   = Due belli occhi (8)
Lauda, anima mea   = Due belli occhi (8)
Pascha concelebranda   = Altri canti di Marte (8)

In Dritter Theil geistlicher Concerten und Harmonien ... colligiret ... durch
Ambrosium Profum (1642):

Haec dicit Deus   = Voi ch'ascoltate in rime sparse
                        (Selva morale e spirituale, 1640)
Heus, bone vir   = Armato il cor (Scherzi musicali,
                        1632)
Spera in Domino   = Io che armato sin hor (ibid.)

In Corollarium geistlicher collectaneorum, berühmter authorum ... gewähret von
Ambrosio Profio (1649):

Alleluja, kommet, jauchzet = Ardo, avvampo (8)
Dein allein ist ja   = Così sol d'una chiara fonte (8)
Frewde, kommet, lasset uns = Ardo, avvampo (8)
    gehen
Longe, mi Jesu   = Parlo, miser, o taccio ? (7)
O Du mächtiger Herr   = Hor che'l ciel e la terra (8)
O Jesu, lindere meinen   = Tu dormi ? (7)
    Schmertzen
O rex supreme   = Al lume della stelle (7)
Resurrexit de sepulcro   = Vago augelletto (8)
Veni, veni, soror mea   = Vago augelletto (8)

APPENDIX C

Achillini, Claudio (1574–1640), jurist and poet, sometime Professor of Civil Law at Bologna. Author of the text of *Mercurio e Marte*, a *torneo* set to music by Monteverdi and performed at Parma in 1628.

Amadino, Ricciardo (late 16th and early 17th cent.), publisher in Venice. He was in partnership with Giacomo Vincenzi from 1583 to 1586 and independent from 1586 to 1621. Monteverdi's *Canzonette* (1584) were published by Vincenzi & Amadino. Amadino alone published all Monteverdi's works from the 3rd book of madrigals (1592) to the 6th book (1614) inclusive.

Andreini, Giovanni Battista (1579–1654), actor, dramatist and poet. Director of a company of actors which had a particular success in Paris. Author of the *sacra rappresentazione*, *La Maddalena*, for which Monteverdi set the prologue.

Andreini, Virginia (1583–1630), wife of the foregoing, actress and singer, known as 'La Florinda'. She sang the title role in the first performance of Monteverdi's *L'Arianna* at Mantua in 1608.

Archilei, Vittoria (née Concarini) (1550–c. 1620), singer and lute-player, wife of the composer and singer Antonio A. She was for many years in the service of the Medici at Florence.

Artusi, Giovanni Maria (c. 1540–1613), theorist and composer, canon of S. Salvatore, Bologna. In his dialogue *Delle imperfettioni della moderna musica* (1600 and 1603) he criticized madrigals which were published in Monteverdi's 4th and 5th books (1603 and 1605).

Badoaro, Giacomo, Venetian nobleman, librettist of Monteverdi's *Le nozze d'Enea con Lavinia* (1641) and *Il ritorno d'Ulisse in patria* (1641) and of Cavalli's *Helena rapita da Teseo* (1653).

Banchieri, Adriano (1568–1634), composer, organist, theorist and poet. A Benedictine monk, he became abbot of the monastery of S. Michele in Bosco (near Bologna) in 1620. He founded the Accademia dei Floridi (later Accademia dei Filomusi) in Bologna in 1614.

Basile, Adriana (c. 1580–*c.* 1640), contralto, known as 'La bella Adriana'. Having made her reputation in Rome and Florence, she was in the service of the Mantuan court from 1610 to 1616 and again from 1623. She married Muzio Baroni. Her daughter Leonora, also a singer, won the admiration of Milton.

Berti, Giovanni Pietro (d. 1638), singer, organist and composer. Tenor at St Mark's, Venice, and second organist from 1624.

Busenello, Giovanni Francesco (1598–1659), lawyer and poet. After studying law at Padua he practised at Venice. Librettist of Monteverdi's *L'incoronazione di Poppea* (1642) and of Cavalli's *Gli amori d'Apollo e di Dafne* (1640), *Didone* (1641), *La prosperità infelice di Giulio Cesare dittatore* (1646) and *Statira, principessa di Persia* (1655).

Caccini, Giulio (c. 1550–1618), singer, lutenist and composer. For many years in the service of the Medici in Florence and a member of Count Bardi's *camerata.*

Cavalli, Pietro Francesco (1602–76), composer and organist. Originally named Caletti-Bruni, he took the name Cavalli from his patron, a Venetian nobleman. He held various posts, as singer, second organist, first organist and finally *maestro di cappella* (1668), at St Mark's, Venice. His first opera, *Le nozze di Teti e di Peleo,* was performed at Venice in 1639.

Chiabrera, Gabriello (1552–1638), lyric and epic poet. Although not attached to any court he enjoyed the favour of Ferdinand I of Tuscany, Carlo Emanuele I of Savoy and the Mantuan court.

Doni, Giovanni Battista (c. 1594–1647), theorist. Originally a student of law, he entered the service of Cardinal Barberini in 1622 and was secretary of the College of Cardinals in Rome from 1629 to 1640. Subsequently Professor of Rhetoric at Florence.

Gabrieli, Andrea (c. 1510–86), organist and composer. At St Mark's, Venice, as second organist (1564) and first organist (1585).

Gabrieli, Giovanni (1557–1613), nephew of the foregoing, organist and composer. In the service of the Duke of Bavaria at Munich, 1575–9. He was appointed second organist of St Mark's, Venice, in 1584, and succeeded his uncle as first organist in 1586.

Gagliano, Marco da (c. 1575–1642), composer. He became *maestro di cappella* of S. Lorenzo, Florence, in 1608 and was made canon in the following year. In 1611 he entered the service of the Medici as *maestro di cappella.* He founded the Accademia degl' Elevati in 1607.

Appendix C—Personalia

Gardano, Angelo (1540–1611), head of a publishing firm in Venice. He published Monteverdi's *Sacrae cantiunculae* (1582) and 1st and 2nd books of madrigals (1587, 1590). After his death the firm was directed by his son-in-law, Bartolomeo Magni, who published Monteverdi's 7th book of madrigals (1619), *Scherzi musicali* (1632) and *Selva morale e spirituale* (1640).

Gastoldi, Giovanni Giacomo (*c.* 1550–1622), composer. *Maestro di cappella* of S. Barbara, Mantua, from 1582, and of Milan Cathedral from 1609.

Gesualdo, Carlo, Prince of Venosa (*c.* 1560–1613), composer. He was a member of one of the oldest families of the Neapolitan nobility.

Giacobbi, Girolamo (1567–1629), composer. He was successively choirboy (1581), singer (1584), *promagister* (1594) and *maestro di cappella* (1604) of S. Petronio, Bologna. His *Andromeda* (1610) was the first opera to be performed at Bologna.

Gombert, Nicolas (*d. c.* 1556), Flemish composer, a pupil of Josquin des Prés. For many years in the service of the Emperor Charles V and canon of Tournai.

Grandi, Alessandro (*d.* 1630), composer. *Maestro di cappella* of S. Spirito, Ferrara, from 1610 to 1617. Singer (1617) and vice-*maestro di cappella* (1620) at St Mark's, Venice. *Maestro di cappella* of S. Maria Maggiore, Bergamo, 1627.

Guarini, Battista (1538–1612), poet and political philosopher. Sometime Professor of Rhetoric and Poetry at Ferrara, and later employed as ambassador at Turin and on other diplomatic missions. His *Il pastor fido* (1580–2) was published in 1589 and first performed in 1595.

Ingegneri, Marc'Antonio (*c.* 1545–92), composer. *Maestro di cappella* of Cremona Cathedral from 1576. Monteverdi was his pupil.

Luzzaschi, Luzzasco (1545–1607), organist and composer. Pupil of Cipriano de Rore and master of Frescobaldi. Organist and *maestro di cappella* to the court of Ferrara.

Magni, Bartolomeo. See *Gardano*.

Marenzio, Luca (1553–99), composer. Successively in the service of several cardinals, of Sigismund III, King of Poland, and of Pope Clement VIII.

Marino, Giambattista (1569–1625), lyric and epic poet and prose writer. He enjoyed the patronage of the courts of Turin and Paris. Several times imprisoned for immorality and criticism of authority.

Martinelli, Caterina (1590–1608), soprano, a pupil of Monteverdi, whose *Lagrime d'amante al sepolcro dell'amata* (published in the 6th book of madrigals, 1614) was written in her memory. She sang in the first performance of Gagliano's *Dafne* (1608).

Martinengo, Giulio Cesare (d. 1613), composer. He followed Croce as *maestro di cappella* of St Mark's, Venice, in 1609 and was succeeded by Monteverdi.

Merula, Tarquinio (c. 1590–1665), composer and organist. *Maestro di cappella* of S. Maria Maggiore, Bergamo (1623 and 1639–52), court organist to Sigismund III of Poland (1624–6), *maestro di cappella* of Cremona Cathedral (1628–39 and from 1652).

Pallavicino, Benedetto (d. 1601), composer. In the service of the Mantuan court from 1582 as a singer. Succeeded de Wert as *maestro di cappella* in 1596 and was succeeded by Monteverdi.

Peri, Jacopo (1561–1633), composer and singer. In the service of the Medici at Florence and a member of Count Bardi's *camerata*. His *Euridice* (1600) is the oldest surviving opera.

Porter, Walter (c. 1595–1659), singer and composer. Tenor in the Chapel Royal under James I and Charles I from 1617, and master of the choristers at Westminster Abbey from 1639.

Raverii, Alessandro (late 16th and early 17th cent.), publisher in Venice, a cousin of Angelo Gardano (*q.v.*). He published reprints of Monteverdi's 1st and 2nd books of madrigals.

Rinuccini, Ottavio (1562–1621), poet, a member of Count Bardi's *camerata* in Florence and for a short time at the court of Henri IV at Paris (1601–3). Librettist of Peri's *Euridice* (1600), Gagliano's *Dafne* (1608; previously set by Peri, 1597) and Monteverdi's *L'Arianna* (1608).

Rovetta, Giovanni (d. 1668), singer and composer. Bass at St Mark's, Venice, from 1623, vice-*maestro di cappella* from 1627, and *maestro di cappella* from 1644.

Saracini, Claudio (b. 1586), composer, member of a noble Sienese family. He held no official appointment and seems to have spent a good deal of time travelling in Italy and elsewhere. A madrigal in his *Seconde musiche* (1620) was dedicated to Monteverdi.

Schütz, Heinrich (1585–1672), composer. He studied law at Marburg and Leipzig. *Kapellmeister* to the Elector of Saxony at Dresden from 1617 to

1639 and again from 1641. He visited Italy in 1609 to study with Giovanni Gabrieli and again in 1628.

Striggio, Alessandro (late 16th and early 17th cent.), poet and violinist, son of the composer Alessandro S. (*c.* 1535–87). Secretary to the court of Mantua, 1622–8. Librettist of Monteverdi's *Orfeo* (1607).

Strozzi, Giulio (1583–*c.* 1660), poet, member of a Florentine family. Librettist of Monteverdi's *Licori finta pazza* (1627) and *Proserpina rapita* (1630).

Tasso, Bernardo (1493–1569), poet. Secretary to Ferrante Sanseverino, Prince of Sorrento, 1536–*c.* 1551. Secretary for criminal affairs to Guglielmo, Duke of Mantua, from 1563.

Tasso, Torquato (1544–95), son of the foregoing, poet. At the court of Ferrara from 1565. In prison from 1579 to 1586. Subsequently in Mantua, Rome, Florence and Naples. Author of the epic poem *Gerusalemme liberata*.

Viadana, Lodovico (1564–1645), composer, so named from his birthplace (original name Grossi). *Maestro di cappella* of Mantua Cathedral, 1594–1609. He became a Franciscan in 1596 and was *maestro di cappella* in Fano from 1610 to 1612.

Vincenti, Alessandro (17th cent.), publisher in Venice. From 1619 to 1665 director of the firm founded by his father Giacomo V. (Vincenzi; see *Amadino*). He published Monteverdi's *Madrigali guerrieri et amorosi* (1638), *Messa a quattro voci et salmi* (1650) and *Madrigali e canzonette* (1651).

Wert, Giaches de (1535–96), composer of Flemish origin, who came to Italy as a boy. He was for many years in the service of the Mantuan court, first as a singer and later as *maestro di cappella* of S. Barbara.

APPENDIX D

BIBLIOGRAPHY

THIS bibliography is in no way complete. It includes only the most important sources for the present study, together with material accessible and of interest to the English reader.

Abert, A. A., 'Claudio Monteverdi und das musikalische Drama'. (Lippstadt, 1954.)

Arnold, D., 'Seconda Prattica, a Background to Monteverdi's Madrigals'. (*Music and Letters*, xxxviii [1957].)

Benvenuti, G., 'Introduction to facsimile edition of *L'incoronazione di Poppea*'. (Milan, 1938.)

Bertolotti, A., 'Musici alla Corte dei Gonzaga in Mantova dal secolo XV al XVIII'. (Milan, 1891.)

Bukofzer, M., 'Music in the Baroque Era'. (New York, 1947.)

Canal, P., 'Della Musica in Mantova, notizie tratte principalmente dall' archivio Gonzaga'. (Venice, 1881.)

Cesari, G., and Pannain, G., 'La musica in Cremona'. (*Istituzioni e monumenti dell' arte musicale italiana*, vi [Milan, 1939].)

Davari, S., 'La Musica a Mantova'. (Mantua, 1884.)

—— 'Notizie biografiche del distinto maestro di musica Claudio Monteverdi'. (Mantua, 1884.)

Einstein, A., 'Abbot Angelo Grillo's Letters as a Source Material for Music History', in *Essays on Music*. (London, 1958.)

—— 'The Italian Madrigal'. (Princeton, 1949.)

Gallico, C., 'Newly Discovered Documents Concerning Monteverdi'. (*Musical Quarterly*, xlviii [1962].)

Goldschmidt, H., 'Studien zur Geschichte der italienischen Oper'. (Leipzig, 1901–4.)

Grout, D. J., 'A Short History of Opera'. (New York, 1947.)

Hughes, C. W., 'Porter, Pupil of Monteverdi'. (*Musical Quarterly*, xx [1934].)

Leichtentritt, H., 'Claudio Monteverdi als Madrigalkomponist'. (*Sammelbände der Internationalen Musikgesellschaft*, xi [1910].)

Malipiero, G. F., 'Claudio Monteverdi'. (Milan, 1930.)

Osthoff, W., 'Das dramatische Spätwerk Claudio Monteverdis'. (Tutzing, 1960.)
—— 'Monteverdi-Funde'. (*Archiv für Musikwissenschaft*, xiv [1957].)

De' Paoli, D., 'Claudio Monteverdi'. (Milan, 1945.)

Prunières, H., 'La Vie et l'œuvre de Claudio Monteverdi'. (Paris, 1924; English edition, London, 1926.)
—— 'Cavalli et l'opéra vénitien au XVIIᵉ siècle'. (Paris, 1931.)

Redlich, H. F., 'Claudio Monteverdi': Bd. I.: Das Madrigalwerk. (Berlin, 1932.)
—— 'Claudio Monteverdi: Life and Works'. (London, 1952.)

Sartori, C., 'Monteverdi'. (Brescia, 1953.)
—— 'Monteverdiana'. (*Musical Quarterly*, xxxviii [1952].)
Schneider, L., 'Claudio Monteverdi: l'homme et son temps'. (Paris, 1921.)
Schrade, L., 'Monteverdi: Creator of Modern Music'. (New York, 1950.)
Solerti, A., 'Gli albori del melodramma'. (Milan, 1905.)
Stevens, D., 'Ornamentation in Monteverdi's Shorter Dramatic Works'. (*Kongressbericht*, Cologne [1958].)

Vogel, E., 'Claudio Monteverdi' (*Vierteljahrsschrift für Musikwissenschaft*, iii [1887].)

Westrup, J. A., 'The Originality of Monteverdi'. (*Proceedings of the Musical Association*, 1934.)
—— 'Monteverdi and the Orchestra'. (*Music and Letters*, xxi [1941].)
—— 'Monteverdi's *Lamento d'Arianna*'. (*The Music Review*, i [1940].)
—— 'Monteverdi and the Madrigal'. (*The Score*, 1949.)
—— 'Two First Performances, Monteverdi's *Orfeo* and Mozart's *La clemenza di Tito*'. (*Music and Letters*, xxxix [1958].)
Worsthorne, S. T., 'Venetian Opera in the Seventeenth Century'. (Oxford, 1954.)

Zimmermann, F. B., 'Purcell and Monteverdi'. (*Musical Times*, July 1958.)

APPENDIX E

DOCUMENTS CONCERNING MONTEVERDI'S LIFE
PREVIOUSLY UNPUBLISHED

Venice, Archivio di Stato

1. *Procuratoria de Supra, Cassier Chiesa, vol. x*

   22 Agosto [1613] ₽ spese diverse // a Cassa, ducati cinquanta, contardi a S. Claudio Monte verde, maestro di cappella ₽ donaficio come nella sua conduta.

   [same day] alli facchini che portavano et riportavano duoi organi a S. Zorgi ₽ il far della prova di S. Claudio Monteverde. mº di Capella.

   2 [ducats] 6 [piccoli] 6 [grossi]

   10 Sett a XX sonatori ordinarij ₽ haver sonato a S. Zorzi il far della prova della messa del nº maestro di Capella, et il giorno di detta prova in chiesa di S. Marco.

   1 [lira] 2 [piccoli] 10 [grossi]

2. *Scuola di S. Rocco*

   (*a*) filza 166, cauzioni (1623–4).
   Polizza de spese fatte ₽ la festa de S. Rocco [1623] ₽ contadij al Sig. Maestro Monte Verde ₽ la festa.

   (L 620.)

   (*b*) filza 168, cauzioni (1627–8).
   Nota dello spese fatte al giorno di Sant' Rocco [1628] contᵃ al S. Claudio, Maestro di Capella.

   (L 146.)

3. *Proc. de Supra, Reg. 193bis, fo. 64–64ᵛ. (Lettere 1594–1620)*

   A letter from the Procurators to the Venetian resident at Milan:

   Essendo venuto a morte il Rᵈº Maestro di Capella della chiesa nostra di S. Marco, ne soño datti proposti diversi soggetti, tra quali il Sʳ Claudio Monteverde Maestro di Capella di S.A. Però la sarà contenta prender informatione del valor, et sufficienza sua, et darne raguaglio, et se le venisse raccordatto qualch altro soggetto, lo receveremo a favore esser particolarm*ᵗᵉ* avisari delle cond*ⁿⁱ* loro, et si off*ᵐᵒ*

Ant° Landi   16 Luglio 1613

In margin: 'fu scritto a Roma, Pad*ᵃ*, Vicenza, Bressa, Berg°, Milā et Mant*ᵃ* alli Residenti.'

4. *Proc. de Supra, Reg. 194, fo. 40ᵛ. (Lettere 1620–36)*

A letter from the Procurators to Monteverdi:

Al maestro di Capella Claudio Monteverde
Molto Mag*ᶜᵒ* S*ʳ*
Habbiamo inteso da una sua quanto V.S. ci avisa, ma ꝑche la sua absentia da q*ᵗᵃ* Capella ꝑ diversi rispetti nō si può più differire, sciamo necessitati à dirgli, ch quante p*ᵐᵃ* si liberi, et ne venghi ad attendere alla sua carica, sapendo massime il termine delle sue obbligationi, et lei beniss° e quanto sij necessaria la sua ꝑsona et carm*ᵗᵉ* la salutiamo.

Ven*ᵃ* li 27 9bre 1627.

5. *Ibid., fo. 50*

A letter from the Procurators to Monteverdi:

Al S. Claudio Monteverde, Parma.
Siamo alle santiss*ᵉ* feste di Natale, et ꝑ honor della Capella di S.M*ᶜᵒ* et satisfat*ᵉ* n̄ra e necess*ᵃ* la v̄ra ꝑsona, vi habbiamo fatto scriver il med*ᵐᵒ* dal S. Rueta, tuttavia habbiamo voluto ancor noi stessi questo tanto farvi sape ꝑch vi disponiate subito alla venuta, acciò giorni così solenni nō si celebrano senza la v̄ra assistenza, conforme alla v̄ra Carica, et vi aspettiamo cō desiderio, cō ch vi salutiamo Caram*ᵗᵉ*.

Ven*ᵃ* a 13 xbre 1628.

6. *Ibid., fo. 81ᵛ*

A letter from the Procurators to Monteverdi, written between August 14 and 18, 1632:

Al S*ʳ* D. Claudio Monteverde m̄ro di Capella d̄lla Ser*ᵐⁱ*.
Sig*ʳⁱ* di Ven.
Ill*ᵐ* et R*ᵈ* S*ʳ*
Riceviamo la sua di 7 Ins*ᵉ*, che altra non nè habbiamo ricevuta et compatiamola sua indispos*ⁿᵉ* passata, et li disturbi delitti che ha tenuto

in q*lle* parte, ma si ralegriamo però che si sij rihavuta, et che sij al fine*mo*, et all'aggiustam*te* delle sue contese, onde staremo quanto prime attendola a ciò possi ritornar al servitio della Chiesa, et al suo carico, conforme a quanto le permette, et e desiderio di cotesti S*i* Ecc*mi*, et n̄ro con che le gli racc*o*.

INDEX

INDEX

Index

Index

Index